Mediterranean Cuisine

Mediterranean Cuisine

Contents

Introduction

Mediterranean cuisine – diverse and international

Mediterranean cuisine includes not only recipes from Italy and Spain but also Turkey, Syria, Lebanon and Israel in the east, Greece and southern France in the north, Morocco and Algeria in the southwest, and Tunisia, Libya and Egypt in the south. Recipes from all of these countries have made their way into this collection.

Fantastic flavours

The early trade routes that evolved hundreds of years ago, linking the lands of Asia and the Mediterranean, allowed the exchange and widespread use of many different herbs and spices, as well as varieties of fruit and vegetables. It is no wonder, then, that Mediterranean cuisine is more than a match for any other regional cooking with its splashes of colour and rich diversity. Yet, despite sharing many spices and flavours, the individual countries have retained their own traditions, so that different types of Mediterranean cuisine have their own clear nuances in appearance, smell and taste. This is evident from even a quick glance at the most famous Mediterranean dishes.

Spain

For centuries the Spanish have enjoyed sitting outside little tapas bars with a glass of wine or sherry and a small bite to eat, soaking up the sun, watching the people pass by and savouring the local cuisine. Typical Spanish recipes like freshly pickled olives or flavoursome mussels with chillies and vegetables are easy and quick to prepare, and ideal for happy gatherings of family and friends.

Italy

With a plethora of starters, homemade pizza and tempting pollo alla Toscana, this book offers you countless opportunities to try out traditional Italian dishes. Yet Italian cuisine also has a number of regional variations, such as Venetian, Florentine, Neapolitan and Sicilian. Each type is bound up with the history, people, climate and geographical conditions of each region.

Turkey

First and foremost, Turkish cuisine centres on fantastic meat-based specialities like lemon and saffron chicken, yoghurt dishes (for example green yoghurt soup), and sumptuous sweets, such as the famous baklava. Many dishes contain traces of the culinary traditions of the old royal palaces and an echo of splendour that is still to be tasted.

Greece

Greek cuisine forms a vital part of this book. We have picked out dishes that you might sample on holiday, such as the world-famous moussaka – healthy recipes that taste absolutely delicious.

France

You can truly dine like a king in France. The country is the world leader in sophisticated cuisine and culinary delectation. And no meal is complete without the obligatory bottle of excellent wine.

A taste tour of the Mediterranean

The recipes in this book will take you on a culinary journey across the whole Mediterranean region. The tastes of past holidays will provide a fond reminder of trips that you have taken. Whether you are cooking family dinners or catering for friends, this collection contains a recipe for every occasion.

Happy cooking and bon appétit!

Starters, soups and snacks

Pumpkin soup
with Parmesan

Serves 4

1 carrot

1 onion

½ stick celery

2 tomatoes

400 g pumpkin

200 g potatoes

2 tbsp olive oil

1 l beef stock

salt

pepper

nutmeg

pinch of Cayenne pepper

50 g grated Parmesan

Preparation time: 20 minutes
Per serving approx. 295 kcal/
1235 kJ
22 g P, 14 g F, 19 g CH

1 Peel the carrot and onion, wash the celery and chop all three vegetables finely. Peel, deseed and chop the tomatoes. Peel the pumpkin and potatoes and cut into cubes.

2 Heat the olive oil in a pan and fry the onion until translucent. Add the carrots and celery and fry. Stir in the tomato and potato and fry before pouring over the beef stock. Season with salt and cook the vegetables for approx. 20 minutes until tender.

3 Strain the soup through a sieve and season with pepper, nutmeg and Cayenne pepper. Bring to a boil and stir in the Parmesan. Serve hot.

Minestrone
with pesto

Serves 4

1.5 l vegetable stock

3 aubergines

100 g courgettes

1 Savoy cabbage

50 g pumpkin

4 tomatoes

100 g green beans

3 potatoes

150 g white beans

30 g dried porcini

2 tbsp olive oil

100 g rice

150 g pesto

salt

pepper

Preparation time: 35 minutes
Per serving approx. 410 kcal/
1717 kJ
16 g P, 11 g F, 59 g CH

1 Soak the porcini in water. Bring the vegetable stock to a boil in a pot. Cut the aubergines and courgettes into cubes, slice the cabbage finely, peel and cube the pumpkin and chop the tomatoes into small pieces. Wash the green beans and slice finely. Peel and dice the potatoes.

2 Add the white beans and the rest of the vegetables to the boiling water. Cut the porcini into small pieces and add to the pot along with the olive oil. Cook the soup for approx. 20 minutes, then add the rice and simmer everything for another 20 minutes. Stir the pesto into the soup before serving and season to taste with salt and pepper.

Bouillabaisse
French fish soup

Serves 4

1 kg mixed ready-to-cook
  fish

1 onion

4 potatoes

4 tomatoes

½ bulb fennel

4 tbsp olive oil

4 bay leaves

herbes de Provence

salt

pepper

4 sachets saffron

4 garlic cloves

500 ml vegetable stock

500 ml fish stock

Preparation time: 25 minutes (plus
cooking and standing time)
Per serving approx. 483 kcal/
2029 kJ
42 g P, 19 g F, 23 g CH

1 Cut the fish into pieces. Peel and chop the onion. Wash, peel and grate the potatoes. Wash the tomato, deseed and cut into dice. Wash the fennel and cut into strips.

2 Heat the olive oil in a pan and braise the onion. Add the potatoes, tomatoes and fennel and fry. Add the bay leaves and season with the herbs and spices. Peel and crush the garlic and add it to the pan. Leave everything to simmer for 10 minutes, then add the fish and cook for another 3 minutes.

3 Heat both the vegetable and the fish stock, mix everything together, remove from the heat and leave the soup to stand for 10 minutes. Garlic bread makes a great accompaniment.

Gazpacho

chilled vegetable soup

Serves 4

400 g ripe tomatoes

1 onion

1 garlic clove

½ cucumber

1 red pepper

1 green pepper

2 slices of white bread

4 tbsp olive oil

2 tbsp sherry vinegar

salt

freshly ground black pepper

Preparation time: 20 minutes (plus standing time)
Per serving approx. 170 kcal/ 710 kJ
4 g P, 11 g F, 14 g CH

1 Score crosses into the tomatoes, scald briefly in boiling water, then douse in cold water and skin. Cut the tomatoes into quarters, deseed and remove the cores. Dice the flesh.

2 Peel the onion and garlic. Wash and peel the cucumber and slice in half lengthways, then cut into 6 cm thick pieces. Wash and halve the peppers, cut out the cores, membranes and seeds, then chop the flesh into bite-sized pieces.

3 Remove a section of the onion and chop it into small dice. Do the same with a quarter of the pepper and a little of the cucumber. Place these vegetables in a separate bowl and set to one side.

4 Blend the rest of the vegetables, onions, garlic and white bread together in a food processor until it is a smooth purée. Stir the olive oil and vinegar into the puréed vegetables. Season to taste with salt and pepper.

5 Cover the soup and leave it to stand in the fridge for at least an hour. Pour the gazpacho into bowls and scatter the finely chopped vegetables over the top.

Red lentil soup
with cumin

Serves 4

200 g red lentils
1 bag soup greens
2 small onions
80 g butter
1 l vegetable stock
250 ml milk
salt
pepper
cumin
a little lemon juice
1 tsp ground paprika

Preparation time: 20 minutes (plus cooking time)
Per serving approx. 415 kcal/
1743 kJ
16 g P, 25 g F, 33 g CH

1 Place the lentils in a fine-meshed sieve, pour water over the top and leave to drain.

2 Wash the soup greens, peel and cut into dice. Peel and dice the onions.

3 Heat half of the butter in a pan until frothy, then fry the onion until it is translucent. Add the chopped soup greens and leave the mixture to simmer for approx. 5 minutes. Add the vegetable stock and lentils, then bring everything to a boil.

4 Boil the soup over a medium heat for approx. 30 minutes, then blend it to a purée, stir in the milk and bring back to the boil. Season to taste with salt, pepper, a pinch of cumin and a little lemon juice.

5 Heat the rest of the butter until it is frothy and stir in the paprika. Warm it for 1 minute, then stir into the soup.

Starters, soups and snacks

Turkish yoghurt soup
with mint

Serves 4

250 g rice

salt

60 g flour

350 g natural yoghurt

2 eggs

1.5 l beef stock

2 tbsp fresh mint

10 g butter

1 tsp paprika

4 tbsp olive oil

Preparation time: 25 minutes
Per serving approx. 623 kcal/
2615 kJ
33 g P, 25 g F, 66 g CH

1 Wash the rice, add it to a pot with 2 litres of salted water, bring to a boil and leave to simmer for approx. 10–15 minutes.

2 Place the flour in a bowl with the yoghurt and eggs, and stir until smooth. Heat the beef stock and stir it into the yoghurt mixture.

3 Take the rice off the heat, drain off any remaining water and leave it to cool a little. Mix the rice with the yoghurt and egg broth and bring everything back to a boil. Season with salt.

4 Wash the mint, shake dry and slice into strips. Heat the butter in a pan and toss the mint briefly in the butter.

5 Mix the paprika with the olive oil. Drizzle the paprika oil over the soup, scatter over the mint and serve.

Green yoghurt soup
with walnuts

Serves 4

2 bunches spring onions

5 tbsp clarified butter

1 kg leaf spinach

1 bunch of parsley

1 bunch of mint

1 bunch of coriander

1 bunch of fresh fenugreek

150 g chopped walnuts

1 l vegetable stock

salt

pepper

800 g natural yoghurt

1–2 tsp freshly grated
   nutmeg

Preparation time: 15 minutes (plus
cooking time)
Per serving approx. 195 kcal/
817 kJ
12 g P, 2 g F, 32 g CH

1 Wash and dry the spring onions, cut into rings and sauté until translucent in the clarified butter.

2 Wash the spinach and herbs and chop roughly. Add to the onions along with the chopped nuts and simmer the mixture for approx. 4 minutes.

3 Pour in the vegetable stock and season the soup with salt and pepper. Cook over a gentle heat for approx. 10 minutes.

4 Remove the soup from the heat and stir in the yoghurt. Ladle into bowls and scatter with the nutmeg.

Spanish-style soup
with chicken

Serves 4

1 ready-to-cook chicken (approx. 1.8 kg)

2 bags soup greens

2 garlic cloves

salt

2 beef tomatoes

2 courgettes

1 Spanish onion

1 tsp dried oregano

150 g spaghetti

1 red pepper

1 green pepper

150 g frozen peas

pepper

paprika

Preparation time: 40 minutes (plus cooking time)
Per serving approx. 992 kcal/ 4153 kJ
66 g P, 61 g F, 40 g CH

1 Cut the chicken in half and place in a pot with the chopped soup greens. Fill the pot with 2 litres of water, add the peeled garlic and bring everything to a boil.

2 Season with salt, half-cover the pot with a lid and simmer over a low heat for approx. 1½ hours.

3 Skin, deseed, core and dice the tomatoes, dice the courgettes and slice the onion into strips.

4 Take the chicken out of the pot, strain the broth through a sieve and then bring it back to a boil. Add the vegetables and the oregano, bring the mixture to a boil, then add the spaghetti and cook according to the packet instructions.

5 Cut the peppers into thin strips. Strip the meat from the chicken and cut into slices. Remove the skin. Add the peppers, peas and meat to the soup and simmer everything for 5 minutes. Season to taste with salt, pepper and paprika.

Bruschetta
with tomatoes

Serves 4

2 garlic cloves

2 beef tomatoes

salt

pepper

½ bunch basil

8 slices white bread or
baguette

6 tbsp olive oil

Preparation time: 25 minutes (plus
baking time)
Per serving approx. 178 kcal/
749 kJ
3 g P, 10 g F, 20 g CH

1 Pre-heat the grill to 200°C (Gas Mark 6, fan oven 180°C). Peel the garlic cloves. Wash and halve the beef tomatoes, remove the cores and seeds, and cut into small dice.

2 Sprinkle the tomato pieces with salt and pepper. Wash the basil, shake dry and tear the leaves from their stalks. Slice the leaves and mix with the tomatoes.

3 Grill the slices of bread on both sides until golden brown. Remove from the grill and rub the sides with the garlic cloves. Drizzle the olive oil over the bread and divide the tomato mixture among the slices.

Beef carpaccio

Serves 4

300 g fillet of beef, fat and
  tendons removed

1 stick celery

2 tbsp lemon juice

6 tbsp olive oil

salt

pepper

50 g Parmesan or Grana
  Padano

Preparation time: 20 minutes
(plus freezing and marinating
time)
Per serving approx. 260 kcal/
1092 kJ
19 g P, 19 g F, 2 g CH

1 Leave the fillet of beef in the freezer for approx. 1 hour until it is slightly frozen, then take out and cut into wafer-thin slices.

2 Wash the celery and cut the green parts into small dice. Mix the lemon juice with oil and salt and stir until it forms a smooth sauce.

3 Place the slices of meat on a plate and sprinkle with freshly ground pepper. Drizzle the sauce over the carpaccio.

4 Leave the carpaccio to stand for approx. 30 minutes, covered with foil. Then scatter shavings of cheese over the meat and add the celery cubes.

Vitello tonnato
veal with tuna sauce

Serves 6

600 g veal (from the shank)
1 stick celery
1 carrot
1 onion
3 cloves
1 bay leaf
500 ml white wine
1 tsp salt
140 g canned tuna
3 anchovy fillets in brine
2 egg yolks
3 tbsp pickled capers
juice of 1 lemon
100 ml olive oil
black pepper

Preparation time: 45 minutes
(plus marinating, cooking and
cooling time)
Per serving approx. 380 kcal/
1590 kJ
26 g P, 25 g F, 7 g CH

1 Wash the veal with cold water and pat dry, then place in a pot. Wash the celery, cut off the green parts and cut into 4 pieces of equal size. Wash the carrot, cut away the top and end, peel and cut into 3 cm lengths. Peel the onion and cut into quarters. Poke the cloves through the bay leaf. Add the spices and the vegetables to the meat along with the white wine. Marinate the meat for 24 hours, turning several times.

2 The next day, pour in enough water to cover the meat. Add salt and bring to a boil. Simmer the meat over a low heat, uncovered, for an hour until cooked, then leave to cool in its broth.

3 Drain the tuna. Rinse the anchovies with cold water and chop roughly. Blend the tuna to a smooth purée with the anchovies, egg yolk, 2 tablespoons of the capers and the lemon juice. Stir in a little of the veal stock and the olive oil, little by little, until you have a velvety sauce. Season with salt and pepper.

4 Slice the veal as finely as possible – a kitchen slicer or electric knife would work best – and arrange on a platter. Pour the tuna sauce over the top and keep cold for at least 2 hours. Scatter over the rest of the capers before serving. White bread goes well with vitello tonnato, especially for dipping in the sauce.

Empanadillas
with mushrooms and prawns

Serves 4

1 pack frozen puff pastry
butter
2 chopped onions
2 chopped tomatoes
1 chopped green pepper
250 g mixed mushrooms
1 tbsp oil
salt
pepper
1 hard boiled egg
100 g ready-to-cook prawns
½ tsp chilli powder
1 egg yolk for coating

Preparation time: 25 minutes
(plus baking time)
Per serving approx. 236 kcal/
992 kJ
12 g P, 16 g F, 12 g CH

1 Leave the puff pastry to thaw. Pre-heat the oven to 200°C (Gas Mark 6, fan oven 180 °C). Heat the butter and fry the onions. Stir in the tomatoes and the pepper. Wash the mushrooms and chop a little, depending on their size. Heat 1 tablespoon of oil in a pan and fry the mushrooms over a high heat. Season with salt and pepper.

2 Peel the egg and chop into small pieces. Chop the prawns into small pieces. Fry the egg and prawns together. Add the chilli and cook the mixture on a low temperature for 10 minutes, stirring occasionally. Season with salt and pepper and leave to cool.

3 Roll out the puff pastry and cut out a circle with a diameter of 15 cm. Place the filling on one half of the circle. Dampen the edges with a little water, fold over and press closed. Brush with the beaten egg yolk and bake for 15 minutes.

Baked tortilla
on skewers

Serves 4

aluminium foil

oil for the tin

1–2 garlic cloves

4 spring onions

1 red pepper

1 green pepper

oil for frying

3 cooked potatoes

5 eggs

75 g sour cream

150 g freshly grated Spanish
   cheese, e.g. Roncal

2 tbsp chives

salt

pepper

wooden skewers for serving

Preparation time: 25 minutes
(plus baking time)
Per serving approx. 523 kcal/
2195 kJ
23 g P, 42 g F, 15 g CH

1 Line a rectangular baking tin (approx. 18 x 25 cm) with aluminium foil and grease with oil. Pre-heat the oven to 180 °C (Gas Mark 4, fan oven 160 °C).

2 Peel and crush the garlic and wash the spring onions and cut into small pieces. Wash and halve the peppers. Remove the seeds and cores and cut the flesh into small dice.

3 Heat a little oil, fry the spring onions and add the crushed garlic. Stir in the peppers, fry everything for approx. 8 minutes, then leave to cool.

4 Cut the potatoes into small dice and mix with the vegetables. Whisk the eggs and mix them with the sour cream, cheese and chives. Fold in the vegetable mixture and add salt and pepper.

5 Pour everything into the baking tin and shake until flat. Bake for approx. 35 minutes in the pre-heated oven at 180 °C (Gas Mark 4, fan oven 160 °C). The tortilla should be cooked all the way through.

6 Take the dish out of the oven, cut into cubes and serve on wooden skewers.

Pickled olives
with garlic and onions

Serves 4

approx. 250 g large olives
(from a jar)
1 large onion
3 garlic cloves
1 bay leaf
3 tbsp red wine vinegar
3 tbsp olive oil

Preparation time: 15 minutes
(plus cooking and standing time)
Per serving approx. 132 kcal/
554 kJ
1 g P, 12 g F, 3 g CH

1 Drain the olives in a sieve. Peel the onion and chop finely. Wash the unpeeled garlic cloves and press flat with the edge of a knife.

2 Cut around the olives lengthways until you hit the stones.

3 Place the olives in a pan with the onion, garlic, bay leaf and vinegar, and pour in water until just covered. Pour the olive oil on top of the water.

4 Bring the contents of the pan to a boil and then leave to simmer for approx. 4–6 hours. Cook the olives until they are done and the water has almost evaporated.

5 Put everything in a jar, seal it tight and leave to stand for several days.

Stuffed dates
with prosciutto

Serves 4

12 fresh dates
125 g mild goat's cheese
1 orange
pinch of Cayenne pepper
sea salt
12 thin slices of prosciutto
12 sprigs rosemary
2 tbsp oil
3 tbsp lemon juice
red peppercorns

Preparation time: 15 minutes
(plus baking time)
Per serving approx. 400 kcal/
1680 kJ
18 g P, 19 g F, 39 g CH

1 Pre-heat the oven to 180 °C (Gas Mark 4, fan oven 160 °C). Pit the dates and score them length-ways. Cut the cheese into 12 pieces.

2 Wash the orange with hot water, then dry it and strip off a little of the peel with a zester. Stuff the dates with the cheese and orange zest. Sprinkle with a little Cayenne pepper and salt.

3 Wrap each date in a slice of prosciutto and stick a sprig of rosemary through it.

4 Arrange the dates on a baking tray, drizzle over a little oil and bake in the oven for 10 minutes.

5 Drizzle the lemon juice over the hot dates, sprinkle with red pepper and serve warm.

Turkish pastries
with yoghurt

Serves 4

400 g flour

1 egg

salt

1 onion

250 g minced beef

1 bunch of freshly chopped
  coriander

pepper

1 tsp mild paprika

pinch of ground cumin

500 g whole milk yoghurt

3 garlic cloves

100 g butter

1 tsp hot paprika

Preparation time: 30 minutes
(plus standing time)
Per serving approx. 773 kcal/
3245 kJ
29 g P, 38 g F, 79 g CH

1 Mix the flour with the egg, ⅛ litre of water and a little salt, and work the mixture into a smooth dough. Wrap the dough in clingfilm and leave to stand for 30 minutes. Peel the onion and chop finely.

2 Mix the minced beef with the onion and coriander, then add some salt, pepper, the mild paprika and cumin and knead the mixture. Divide the dough into 5 pieces and roll out until they are 2 mm thick. Cut into squares with 4 cm long sides.

3 Place a little of the beef mixture on each pastry square. Join the edges together in the middle. Boil in salted water for 4–5 minutes until the pastries rise to the surface. Leave to dry off.

4 Strain the yoghurt through a muslin cloth and leave to drain. Peel and crush the garlic. Heat the butter and add the hot paprika. Mix the yoghurt and garlic together and season with salt and pepper.

5 Drizzle the paprika butter over the pastries and serve with yoghurt.

Chicken falafel
with yoghurt

Serves 4

50 g bulgur wheat

4 large, ready-made tortillas

baking parchment

250 g canned chickpeas

3 chopped spring onions

1 chopped gherkin

2 finely chopped tomatoes

3 tbsp chopped flat-leaf parsley

2 tbsp freshly chopped mint

1 tbsp lemon juice

2 tbsp olive oil

1–2 chopped garlic cloves

1 chopped shallot

1 tsp ground coriander

1 tsp ground cumin

½ tsp ground cinnamon

400 g minced chicken

salt

pepper

flour for coating

oil for deep frying

100 g yoghurt

Preparation time: 35 minutes
(plus baking and deep frying time)
Per serving approx. 370 kcal/
1554 kJ
34 g P, 10 g F, 34 g CH

1 Soak the bulgur wheat in hot water for approx. 20 minutes. Cut the tortillas into 3 wedges each and cover with a damp tea-towel to prevent them from drying out. Cut the baking parchment into 12 rectangles, each approx. 7 x 16 cm. Wrap the baking parchment around the lower half of the tortillas to form a kind of bag. Twist the ends of the paper.

2 Place the bulgur wheat in a sieve and press out the water. Drain the chick peas and mix them with the bulgur wheat, spring onions, gherkin, tomatoes, herbs, lemon juice and 1 tablespoon of olive oil. Fry the garlic with the shallot in the rest of the oil until translucent. Add the spices and sauté until they begin to smell fragrant. Combine the mixture with the minced meat and add salt and pepper. With damp hands, form small patties, coat them in flour, and deep fry them in hot oil for approx. 5 minutes. Place a falafel, some of the bulgur mixture and some yoghurt in each of the baking parchment parcels and serve.

Yufka pastries
with sheep's cheese

Serves 6

200 g sheep's cheese
1 bunch dill
1 bunch flat-leaf parsley
butter for greasing
12 yufka pastry sheets
salt
2 tbsp olive oil
150 g butter
140 ml milk

Preparation time: 20 minutes
(plus cooking and baking time)
Per serving approx. 1103 kcal/
4631 kJ
16 g P, 97 g F, 45 g CH

1 Crush the sheep's cheese. Wash the herbs, shake dry and chop finely. Mix the herbs into the cheese. Grease a large baking tin.

2 Cut the yufka pastry sheets to the dimensions of the tin. Place one sheet in the tin. Pre-heat the oven to 225 °C (Gas Mark 7, fan oven 200 °C).

3 Heat some salted water in a pan with the olive oil and boil 10 pastry sheets individually, for approx. 2 minutes each. Spoon them out when they float to the surface. Plunge them into cold water straight away, and then leave to dry.

4 Melt the butter and stir in the milk. Brush the pastry sheets with the mixture and layer 5 sheets on top of one another in the tin. Spoon the cheese mixture over the sheets, then place the remaining 5 sheets on top.

5 Fold the overhanging pastry edges inwards. Place the last uncooked pastry sheet on top and dab with the butter and milk mixture.

6 Cut the pastries into 8 x 8 cm squares and bake in the oven for 30 minutes. Serve hot.

Tuna tramezzini
with capers

Serves 4

140 g canned tuna in brine

2 anchovy fillets in brine

1 tbsp pickled capers

2 tbsp double cream cheese

4 tbsp lemon juice

salt

black pepper

16 slices white sandwich
bread

Preparation time: 20 minutes
(plus cooking time)
Per serving approx. 691 kcal/
2902 kJ
17 g P, 31 g F, 79 g CH

1 Drain the tuna and flake it roughly with a fork. Drain the anchovies and capers. Rinse the anchovies under cold running water. Chop the capers and anchovies roughly with a large kitchen knife. Put the tuna, anchovies and capers in a bowl, add the cream cheese and lemon juice and stir until the mixture is smooth. Season to taste with salt and pepper.

2 Cut the crusts off the slices of bread. Spread 8 slices with the tuna paste. Place the other slices on top and press down lightly. Slice the tramezzini diagonally and arrange on plates.

Stuffed vine leaves
with minced meat

Serves 4

500 g pickled vine leaves

50 g prunes

50 g pickled stoneless sour
   cherries

50 g raisins

250 g minced beef

100 g rice

3 tbsp finely chopped parsley

pinch of ground saffron

1 tbsp freshly chopped mint
   leaves

freshly ground black pepper

salt

2 untreated lemons

125 ml olive oil

Preparation time: 30 minutes
(plus soaking and cooking time)
Per serving 453 kcal/1901 kJ
5 g P, 27 g F, 46 g CH

1 Soak the vine leaves in cold water for approx. 6 hours, then leave to dry thoroughly on kitchen paper. Unfold the leaves so that the underside is facing upwards, then cut off the stems.

2 Chop the prunes, cherries and raisins roughly and mix with the minced meat, rice, parsley and the other herbs and spices. Place a tablespoon of the mixture on each vine leaf. Fold the edges together and then fold the side edges inwards. The stuffed vine leaves should be approx. 5 cm long.

3 Slice the lemons and cover the bottom of a pan with half of the slices. Place the vine leaves on top. Cover with the rest of the lemon slices. Pour over the olive oil and 2 cups of water, cover the pan and simmer over a medium heat for an hour.

4 Remove the lemon slices and sprinkle the stuffed vine leaves with the juice. Leave to cool and then serve.

Tabbouleh
Lebanese bulgur salad

Serves 4

200 g bulgur wheat

1 bunch flat-leaf parsley

4 sprigs fresh mint

½ Chinese cucumber

4 spring onions

2 beef tomatoes

juice of 2 lemons

4 tbsp olive oil

salt

black pepper

Preparation time: 30 minutes
(plus standing time)
Per serving approx. 308 kcal/
1291 kJ
6 g P, 13 g F, 42 g CH

1 Boil the bulgur wheat in 500 ml water for approx. 10 minutes, then remove from the hob and leave to stand for 20 minutes.

2 Meanwhile, wash the parsley and mint, shake dry and chop. Peel the cucumber and cut into small dice. Wash the spring onions and chop finely.

3 Wash the tomatoes, remove the cores and chop the flesh finely.

4 Fluff up the bulgur wheat with a fork. Mix with the salad vegetables and herbs in a bowl.

5 Mix the lemon juice and oil with salt and pepper and pour over the salad. Leave to stand for at least an hour, then stir thoroughly once more and serve.

Pasta, rice and grains

Spaghetti bolognese
a classic dish

Serves 4

1 onion

1 garlic clove

75 g streaky bacon

1 carrot

½ stick celery

2 tbsp olive oil

400 g minced meat

100 ml red wine

salt

pepper

100 ml milk

1 tsp freshly chopped
oregano

400 g chopped tinned
tomatoes

1 tbsp sugar

400 g spaghetti

50 g grated Parmesan

thyme for garnishing

Preparation time: 30 minutes
(plus cooking time)
Per serving approx. 733 kcal/
3069 kJ
41 g P, 28 g F, 76 g CH

1 Peel and chop the onion and garlic. Cut the bacon into cubes. Peel the carrot, wash the celery, and cube both. Heat the oil and fry the bacon. Add the vegetables and then the mince, and fry until the meat is brown, stirring constantly.

2 Pour in the red wine and leave the mixture to simmer until the liquid has boiled off. Season with salt and pepper. Stir in the milk, and boil the sauce down until it is smooth. Stir the oregano, tomatoes and sugar into the sauce and cook everything until tender over a low heat for approx. 30 minutes.

3 In the meantime, cook the spaghetti until *al dente* according to the packet instructions, then drain. Transfer to plates, divide the sauce between the spaghetti, sprinkle over the Parmesan and serve garnished with thyme.

Bucatini
with Gorgonzola and ham

Serves 4

400 g bucatini

150 g Gorgonzola

250 ml cream

salt

pepper

sugar

150 g slices Parma ham

1 bunch parsley

Preparation time: 25 minutes
Per serving approx. 905 kcal/
3789 kJ
35 g P, 46 g F, 87 g CH

1 Cook the bucatini according to the packet instructions. Remove the Gorgonzola rind, cut the cheese into cubes and melt in a wide pan over a low heat.

2 Stir in the cream, season with salt, pepper and sugar, and leave the mixture to boil down for approx. 3–5 minutes, stirring occasionally.

3 Cut the slices of ham in half and warm in the cheese sauce. Wash, dry and finely chop the parsley.

4 Mix the bucatini with the Gorgonzola sauce and serve sprinkled with the parsley.

Spaghetti
with pesto

Serves 4

1 tbsp pine nuts

1½ bunch basil

1 garlic clove

salt

3 tbsp Parmesan

60 ml olive oil

pepper

500 g spaghetti

Preparation time: 30 minutes
Per serving approx. 518 kcal/
2169 kJ
17 g P, 11 g F, 86 g CH

1 Toast the pine nuts in a dry pan. Tear the basil leaves from their stalks, then wash and dry. Peel the garlic and chop roughly together with the pine nuts and basil.

2 Blend the basil, garlic, pine nuts and salt to a paste. Stir in the Parmesan and olive oil, and season with pepper.

3 In the meantime, cook the spaghetti in plenty of salted water according to the packet instructions, until *al dente*. Mix with the pesto and serve.

Ravioli
with mushroom stuffing

Serves 4

400 g flour

5 eggs

salt

400 g mushrooms

40 g butter

1 garlic clove

100 g onions

100 ml white wine

1 bunch flat-leaf parsley

½ bunch thyme

pepper

100 g ricotta

40 g Parmesan

4 tbsp olive oil

300 g tomatoes

2 tbsp chives

Preparation time: 35 minutes
(plus resting and cooking time)
Per serving approx. 714 kcal/
2989 kJ
26 g P, 30 g F, 77 g CH

1 Mix the flour, 4 eggs, 1 teaspoon of salt and 1–2 tablespoons of water together to form a stretchy dough. Wrap in cling film and place in the fridge to cool for 30 minutes. Heat the butter, dice the mushrooms and fry for 3 minutes in the butter. Add the chopped garlic clove and 100 g of the chopped onions and fry for 2–3 minutes. Deglaze the pan with the wine. Add the bunch of parsley and the chopped leaves of the ½ bunch of thyme, and cook for another 3 minutes. Season with salt and pepper and leave to cool.

2 Separate one of the eggs. Mix the mushroom mixture with the ricotta, 20 g finely grated Parmesan and an egg yolk. Roll the dough out on a floured surface until it is about the thickness of 2 plates (2–3 mm) and cut it into 4 wide strips, each about 10 cm thick. Spoon the filling onto 2 of the strips every 3–4 cm, leaving about 1 cm free around the edges. Whisk the egg white with 2 tablespoons of water, and brush it between the mounds of filling. Place the remaining strips of dough on top of the first two, press down lightly around the filling and cut through the areas in between with a pastry wheel.

3 Cook the ravioli for 6–8 minutes until *al dente*, then fry briefly in olive oil. Skin and dice the tomatoes, add them to the ravioli, fry for 1 minute, and then add salt and pepper. Grate the rest of the Parmesan over the top, and serve sprinkled with the chives.

Spaghetti
al pomodoro

Serves 4

400 g spaghetti

salt

1–1.5 kg ripe beef tomatoes

2 shallots

1 small chilli

pepper

6 tbsp olive oil

12 fresh basil leaves

200 g mozzarella

Preparation time: 30 minutes
Per serving approx. 553 kcal/
2315 kJ
25 g P, 16 g F, 76 g CH

1 Cook the spaghetti in salted water until *al dente*, according to the packet instructions. Score the tops of the tomatoes with crosses and remove the stalk, cover with boiling water, then take out, skin, deseed and cut the flesh into dice.

2 Peel and chop the shallots. Deseed the chilli and cut into thin strips. Mix the shallots and chilli together, season with salt and pepper, and add the olive oil. Wash and dry the basil leaves and chop. Add the shallot mixture and basil to the tomatoes.

3 Cut the mozzarella into 2 cm cubes. Drain the spaghetti and leave to dry. Place in a cooking pot and toss with the tomatoes and cubes of mozzarella. Heat gently, turning, for 2–3 minutes, until the mozzarella is beginning to melt.

Pasta

with sardines

Serves 4

8 sardine fillets

1 bulb fennel

2 garlic cloves

½ red chilli

4 tbsp olive oil

350 g linguine

salt

zest of 1 untreated lemon

1 tbsp lemon juice

2 tbsp toasted pine nuts

3 tbsp freshly chopped
  parsley

pepper

Preparation time: 30 minutes
Per serving approx. 458 kcal/
1917 kJ
23 g P, 12 g F, 62 g CH

1 Wash, dry and roughly chop the sardine fillets. Wash the fennel bulb and slice into thin strips. Peel the garlic and cut into thin slices. Wash, dry and finely dice the chilli.

2 Heat 2 tablespoons of the olive oil, add the garlic and chilli and fry, then add the fennel, frying for another 5 minutes and then mixing in the sardines. Cook for another 4 minutes.

3 Cook the pasta in plenty of salted water according to the packet instructions until *al dente*, then drain thoroughly. Mix the lemon zest and juice, pine nuts, parsley, salt and pepper into the sardines. Add to the pasta along with the rest of the oil and mix everything together.

Pappardelle
with hare ragout

Serves 4

400 g ready-to-cook hare
   meat

50 g pancetta

1 onion

1 stick celery

1 carrot

1 beef tomato

2 tbsp olive oil

salt

pepper

½ tsp dried thyme

100 ml dry white wine

125 ml beef stock

400 g pappardelle

Preparation time: 30 minutes
(plus braising time)
Per serving approx. 615 kcal/
2575 kJ
21 g P, 23 g F, 76 g CH

1 Chop the meat into small pieces and the pancetta into little cubes. Peel and chop the onion. Wash, peel and slice the celery and carrot.

2 Score crosses into the beef tomato, cover with boiling water, then skin and chop the flesh.

3 Heat the oil in a pan and fry the cubes of pancetta. Add the hare meat and fry well on all sides. Add the celery, carrot and tomato, and season with salt, pepper and thyme. Add the wine and stock, cover the pot, and simmer the ragout at a low temperature for approx. 1 hour and 20 minutes.

4 While the ragout is cooking, boil the pappardelle in plenty of salted water until *al dente*, then drain thoroughly. Mix the pasta into the hare ragout and serve.

Pasta

with aubergines

Serves 4

3 aubergines

5–6 tbsp oil

1 garlic clove

1 shallot

2 tbsp lemon juice

4 tbsp olive oil

150 g yoghurt

salt

pepper

400 g tagliatelle

100 g firm ricotta

½ bunch chives

Preparation time: 45 minutes
Per serving approx. 443 kcal/
1855 kJ
18 g P, 8 g F, 74 g CH

1 Pre-heat the oven to 225 °C (Gas Mark 7, fan oven 200 °C). Wash and dry the aubergines. Brush two of the aubergines with half of the oil, and bake for approx. 30 minutes on the middle shelf of the oven until the skin is black. Scrape the aubergine flesh from the skin.

2 Peel the garlic clove and the shallot and blend to a fine purée with the aubergine, lemon juice and 4 tablespoons of olive oil. Stir in the yoghurt and season to taste with salt and pepper.

3 Cook the tagliatelle. Crumble the ricotta. Slice the third aubergine.

4 Heat the rest of the olive oil and brown the aubergine slices lightly on both sides.

5 Wash the chives, dry and cut into lengths. Drain the pasta, refresh in cold water and leave to dry.

6 Mix together the tagliatelle, aubergine slices and cheese. Serve with the sauce and sprinkle over the chives.

Polenta slices
with beef

Serves 4

200 g polenta
salt
1 onion
2 courgettes
2 tbsp olive oil
300 g minced beef
30 g cubed ham
black pepper
4 tbsp tomato purée
40 g butter
20 g freshly grated
   Parmesan

Preparation time: 20 minutes
(plus cooking time)
Per serving approx. 500 kcal/
2090 kJ
24 g P, 27 g F, 41 g CH

1 Gradually add the polenta to 1 litre of boiling salted water, stirring constantly with a wooden spoon. Keep the water temperature under the boiling point to prevent lumps from forming. Once all the polenta has been added, lower the temperature and leave to simmer for approx. 30 minutes, stirring briskly. If the mixture becomes too firm while stirring, add boiling water by the tablespoonful; if it is too runny, stir in some more polenta.

2 Turn the finished polenta out onto a large wooden board or a towel sprinkled with semolina, smooth down until it is 5 cm thick and leave to cool.

3 Chop the onion finely. Wash the courgettes and cut into ½ cm thick slices. Heat the oil in a pan and fry the onion until translucent. Add the minced beef and ham cubes and fry until brown and crumbly. Add salt and pepper and stir in the tomato purée and 4 tablespoons of water. Add the courgette slices and simmer everything for approx. 5 minutes. Pre-heat the oven to 150 °C (Gas Mark 2, fan oven 130 °C).

4 Grease a large, shallow ovenproof dish with the melted butter. Cut the firm polenta into 1 cm thick slices. Lay the slices in the dish. Drizzle over the rest of the butter, sprinkle over a few table-spoons of Parmesan and cover with the meat sauce. Bake for approx. 30 minutes on the middle shelf of the oven. Sprinkle once more with Parmesan before serving.

Risotto milanese
with saffron

Serves 4

1 onion

50 g butter

50 ml dry white wine

400 g risotto rice (e.g. Arborio)

1 l vegetable stock

½ tsp saffron threads

50 g freshly grated Parmesan

Preparation time: 15 minutes (plus cooking time)
Per serving approx. 548 kcal/ 2300 kJ
12 g P, 19 g F, 80 g CH

1 Peel and finely chop the onion. Melt 2 tablespoons of butter in a large pot and fry the onion. Add the wine to the onion and cook over a medium heat until the liquid has almost completely boiled down.

2 Add the rice to the pot and fry, stirring, for approx. 1 minute, until it is coated with the butter. Add the stock little by little, and leave to boil down. Only add more stock once what is in the pot has been absorbed by the rice.

3 The rice will be half-cooked after approx. 10 minutes. Stir the saffron threads into the remaining stock and add to the rice.

4 Simmer for another 15 minutes until the rice is creamy yet still firm to the bite.

5 Stir the rest of the butter and the cheese into the rice, cover, and leave the risotto to stand for a few minutes. Ladle onto plates and serve with Parmesan.

Risotto
with porcini

Serves 4

250 g fresh (or 50 g dried) porcini

1 onion

3 tbsp butter

400 g risotto rice

1 l hot vegetable stock

50 ml white wine

salt

pepper

50 g Parmesan

2 tbsp freshly chopped parsley

Preparation time: 30 minutes
Per serving approx. 498 kcal/
2092 kJ
14 g P, 12 g F, 80 g CH

1 Clean the fresh porcini and cut into small pieces. If using dried porcini, soak in 200 ml water. Peel and chop the onion. Heat 2 tablespoons of butter in a pan and sauté the onion and porcini. Add the risotto rice and cook a little longer until the rice looks slightly glassy.

2 Gradually add the vegetable stock and white wine (or 750 ml stock, the wine and the water used for soaking the porcini) until the rice has completely absorbed all the liquid and is creamy. Season with salt and pepper. Grate the Parmesan and stir it into the risotto with the rest of the butter and parsley, then serve.

Classic lasagne
typically Italian

Serves 4

100 g streaky bacon
1 tbsp olive oil
1 onion
2 garlic cloves
350 g mixed mince meat
salt
pepper
paprika
150 ml red wine
500 g peeled plum tomatoes
2 tbsp butter
2 tbsp flour
500 ml milk
nutmeg
500 g lasagne sheets (no
  precooking required)
100 g freshly grated
  Parmesan
butter for greasing the
  baking dish

Preparation time: 30 minutes
(plus baking time)
Per serving approx. 1125
kcal/4710 kJ
45 g P, 64 g F, 91 g CH

1 Cut the bacon into cubes. Heat the oil and fry the bacon cubes. Chop the onion and garlic cloves finely, add to the bacon and fry. Add the minced meat and cook until crumbly, stirring constantly. Season with salt, pepper and paprika, and pour in the red wine. Add the peeled tomatoes with their juice and simmer everything for approx. 10–15 minutes.

2 Make a roux out of the melted butter and the flour, adding the milk. Bring to a boil, stirring, and add salt, pepper and nutmeg. Pour a little of the béchamel sauce into a greased baking dish. Then alternate layers of lasagne sheets, meat sauce and béchamel sauce until the dish is full.

3 Scatter over the grated cheese, cover, and bake in the oven at 180 °C (Gas Mark 4, fan oven 160 °C) for 20 minutes, then uncover and cook for another 10 minutes. Serve with salad.

Cannelloni
with spinach

Serves 4

300 g flour

3 eggs

salt

3 onions

2 garlic cloves

1 tbsp clarified butter

500 g minced meat

400 g spinach

pepper

½ bunch spring onions

2 carrots

2 sticks celery

2 tbsp olive oil

1 egg white

100 g butter

10 g Parmesan

10 g breadcrumbs

Preparation time: 20 minutes
(plus standing and baking time)
Per serving approx. 870 kcal/
3654 kJ
43 g P, 50 g F, 62 g CH

1 Mix the flour, eggs, salt and a little water to form a smooth dough. Wrap in foil and set aside in a cool place for approx. 30 minutes.

2 Peel and finely chop the onions and garlic cloves. Heat the clarified butter in a pan and fry the onion and garlic until they are translucent. Add the minced meat and cook until it is crumbly. Cover and simmer over a gentle heat for approx. 3–5 minutes.

3 Wash and chop the spinach. Add to the pan and let it wilt, then season with salt and pepper. Set the pan to one side.

4 Wash the spring onions and slice into rings. Peel the carrot, wash the celery, and dice both. Sauté the vegetables for 3–5 minutes in 2 table-spoons of hot olive oil, then stir into the meat mixture.

5 Pre-heat the oven to 200 °C (Gas Mark 6, fan oven 180 °C). Roll out the pasta dough and cut out 4 sheets, each 15 cm x 20 cm. Divide half of the meat mixture between the sheets. Brush the edges with egg white, roll up the sheets, and cut into pieces approximately 4 cm wide each. Spoon the rest of the filling into a greased baking dish and place the cannelloni on top.

6 Melt the butter in a small pan and pour it over the cannelloni. Grate the Parmesan, mix with the breadcrumbs, scatter over the cannelloni and bake in the oven for approx. 10 minutes. Serve immediately.

Spanish paella
a classic dish

Serves 4

200 g deep frozen squid
   rings
1 onion
2 garlic cloves
2 small red chillies
1 red pepper
1 green pepper
4 chicken legs
salt
black pepper
pinch of paprika
200 g chorizo (or spicy
   sausages)
4 tbsp olive oil
250 g parboiled rice
100 ml white wine
1 small packet of saffron
   (0.2 g)
approx. 500 ml chicken stock
1 untreated lemon

Preparation time: 30 minutes
(plus thawing and cooking time)
Per serving approx. 850 kcal/
3550 kJ
51 g P, 43 g F, 59 g CH

1 Leave the squid rings to thaw. Peel and finely chop the onion and garlic cloves. Wash the chillies and peppers and pat dry, the cut in half lengthways. Finely chop the chillies and cut the peppers into 1 cm pieces.

2 Rinse the chicken legs in cold water, pat dry and rub with salt, pepper and paprika. Skin the sausages and cut into slices.

3 Heat a little oil in a large pan with steep sides. Add the chicken legs and fry over a high heat, approx. 3 minutes on each side, then remove from the pan. Add the rest of the oil to the chicken fat, then add the chopped onion, garlic, chilli and pepper and fry, stirring constantly. Pour in the rice and mix until it looks glassy.

4 Deglaze the vegetable and rice mixture with the white wine. Stir in the saffron. Add salt and pepper, pour in approx. 500 ml of chicken stock and bring to a boil, before adding the chicken legs. Cover the pan and cook for approx. 15 minutes.

5 Top up with stock if necessary to prevent the rice from catching. Add the thawed squid rings and chorizo slices to the paella and cook everything for another 15 minutes. Season everything once again with salt, pepper and paprika. Wash the lemon, cut into eight wedges and serve with the paella.

Sweet-and-sour couscous
with raisins and lemons

Serves 4

250 g couscous

3 lemons

100 g raisins

125 ml apple juice

600 g tomatoes

50 g almond flakes

150 ml tomato juice

1 tbsp oil

cinnamon

freshly grated nutmeg

salt

pepper

2 sprigs fresh mint

Preparation time: 15 minutes
(plus cooking and cooling time)
Per serving approx. 473 kcal/
1985 kJ
12 g P, 11 g F, 76 g CH

1 Cook the couscous according to the packet instructions, then leave to cool. Squeeze 2 of the lemons and mix the juice into the cooled couscous.

2 Pour the apple juice into a small bowl and soak the raisins in the juice. Score crosses into the tomatoes and plunge briefly into boiling water. Remove them from the water, remove their skins, cut in half and cut into cubes.

3 Toast the almond flakes in a dry pan until golden brown. Mix the tomato pieces and tomato juice with the oil, the soaked raisins and the toasted almonds, add to the couscous and fold everything together thoroughly.

4 Season the couscous with a little cinnamon, the freshly grated nutmeg, salt and pepper. Wash the mint, shake dry and tear the leaves from their stalks. Tear them into smaller pieces and mix into the couscous.

5 Wash the remaining lemon with hot water, dry, and slice very thinly. Garnish the couscous with the lemon slices and leave to stand for 30 minutes before serving.

Red meat and poultry

Fillet of beef
with red wine and herbs

Serves 4

500 g potatoes
500 g courgettes
500 g tomatoes
500 g chanterelles
1 onion
1 garlic clove
4 tbsp olive oil
1.5 kg fillet of beef
salt
pepper
150 ml red wine
50 ml port
3 sprigs thyme
3 sprigs rosemary
3 sprigs sage
4 bay leaves
200 g crème fraîche

Preparation time: 30 minutes
(plus braising time)
Per serving approx. 857 kcal/
3588 kJ
89 g P, 37 g F, 31 g CH

1 Peel the potatoes. Slice the courgettes and potatoes. Skin and slice the tomatoes. Cut the chanterelles into small pieces. Peel and roughly chop the onion and the garlic clove.

2 Heat the oil in a casserole dish and brown the meat well on all sides. Season with salt and pepper. Add the vegetables to the meat, and pour over the red wine and port. Tie the herbs together and place on top of the meat. Cover the dish, and braise in the oven at 200 °C (Gas Mark 6, fan oven 180 °C) for approx. 45 minutes. Once the cooking time is up, take the meat and herbs out and keep the meat warm.

3 Stir the crème fraîche into the roasting juices and season to taste. Serve the sauce with the meat.

Lamb
with tomatoes and garlic

Serves 4

2 garlic cloves

1 sprig rosemary

1 kg lamb

2 tbsp flour

60 ml olive oil

175 ml white wine

salt

pepper

400 g tomatoes

120 ml lamb stock

Preparation time: 25 minutes
(plus braising time)
Per serving approx. 583 kcal/
2441 kJ
75 g P, 25 g F, 6 g CH

1 Peel and chop the garlic cloves. Tear the rosemary leaves from their stems and chop. Wash the lamb, pat dry and cut into cubes. Coat with flour.

2 Heat the oil in a casserole dish and sauté the garlic and rosemary. Add the cubes of lamb and brown thoroughly on all sides, then remove and keep warm. Deglaze with the wine, bring the mixture to a boil and then add the meat once again. Season with salt and pepper.

3 Skin, deseed and dice the tomatoes, and add to the dish along with the lamb stock. Cover the dish and braise for approx. 1 hour 30 minutes in the oven at 180 °C (Gas Mark 4, fan oven 160 °C). Serve with fresh French bread.

Chicken
Tuscan-style

Serves 4

1 chicken (approx. 1.2 kg)

salt

pepper

1 onion

2 red peppers

1 garlic clove

15 ml olive oil

300 g tomato passata

150 ml dry white wine

1 sprig oregano

400 g tinned cannellini beans

3 tbsp white breadcrumbs

Preparation time: 20 minutes
(plus braising time)
Per serving approx. 685 kcal/
2868 kJ
69 g P, 34 g F, 20 g CH

1 Cut the chicken into 8 pieces and season with salt and pepper. Peel and slice the onion, deseed the peppers and slice into rings, and peel and chop the garlic clove.

2 Heat the oil in a casserole dish and brown the chicken pieces on all sides. Remove from the dish and keep warm.

3 Braise the onion slices, pepper rings and garlic in the cooking fat. Return the chicken pieces to the dish and add the tomatoes, wine and oregano. Bring to a boil, then cover and leave to simmer for approx. 35 minutes. After 30 minutes stir in the beans and warm through. Scatter the breadcrumbs over the dish and place under a hot grill until golden brown.

Roast rabbit
with anchovies

Serves 4

1.5 kg ready-to-cook boneless rabbit

4 slices Parma ham

25 anchovy fillets from a jar

pepper

100 g freshly grated Parmesan

salt

150 g smoked bacon

2 tbsp olive oil

12 shallots

500 ml dry white wine

5 tomatoes

Preparation time: 30 minutes (plus braising time)
Per serving approx. 775 kcal/ 3245 kJ
95 g P, 41 g F, 4 g CH

1 Spread out the meat on a worktop and place the Parma ham on top. Rinse the anchovy fillets, pat dry, chop 20 of the anchovies and distribute them on the rabbit, then sprinkle over pepper and Parmesan.

2 Roll up the rabbit and tie securely with cooking twine. Rub the outside with salt and pepper. Remove the rind from the bacon and cut into cubes. Heat the oil in a pot and brown the meat thoroughly on all sides, then remove from the pot and set to one side. Fry the bacon and the peeled whole shallots in the roasting fat.

3 Return the meat to the pot, pour in the wine and 100 ml water, cover, and braise in the oven at 160 °C (Gas Mark 3, fan oven 140 °C) for approx. 30 minutes, turning once.

4 Skin, deseed and dice the tomatoes, and add to the rabbit along with the rest of the anchovies once the meat has cooked for 30 minutes. Braise everything for another 20 minutes. Season the sauce with salt and pepper, and serve the meat cut into slices.

Roast chicken
with fennel

Serves 4

1 ready-to-cook roasting
   chicken (approx. 1.5 kg)

salt

1 onion

120 ml olive oil

2 fennel bulbs

1 garlic clove

pinch of ground nutmeg

pepper

4 thin slices pancetta

120 ml dry white wine

Preparation time: 30 minutes
(plus roasting time)
Per serving approx. 845 kcal/
3538 kJ
66 g P, 61 g F, 4 g CH

1 Rub the inside of the chicken with salt, and stuff it with the quartered onion. Rub the outside with 45 ml of olive oil and place in a large casserole dish, breast side up. Mix the chopped green parts of the fennel with the peeled and chopped garlic clove, nutmeg, salt and pepper, and rub into the chicken. Lay the slices of pancetta over the chicken breast, drizzle with 30 ml of olive oil and roast in the oven at 180 °C (Gas Mark 3, fan oven 160 °C) for approx. 30 minutes.

2 Cook the fennel bulbs in boiling water until *al dente*, and cut into quarters. Turn the chicken, place the fennel around it and drizzle over the rest of the olive oil. Pour over 60 ml of the wine and roast everything for another 30 minutes. Finally, turn the chicken again, pour over the rest of the wine and roast for another 15 minutes until the meat is cooked through.

Florentine steak
grilled to perfection

Serves 4

4 beef steaks, with bone
(approx. 400 g each)

salt

pepper

Preparation time: 15 minutes
Per serving approx. 295 kcal/
1235 kJ
44 g P, 13 g F, 1 g CH

1 Wash the steaks and pat dry. Grill for approx. 5 minutes on an open grill or using the oven grill until they have a good crust. Turn the steaks and grill the other side until crispy. The inside should still be rare.

2 Season the meat with salt and pepper. Serve hot with fresh bread and a mixed green salad.

Escalopes in Marsala sauce

Serves 4

4 pork escalopes

salt

pepper

4 tbsp flour

3 tbsp clarified butter

75 ml Marsala

50 ml beef stock

Preparation time: 10 minutes
(plus frying time)
Per serving approx. 572 kcal/
2404 kJ
41 g P, 33 g F, 28 g CH

1 Beat the escalopes flat. Rub them with salt and pepper and coat with the flour.

2 Heat the clarified butter in a pan and fry the escalopes for 4 minutes on each side, then remove from the pan and keep warm.

3 Deglaze the meat juice with the Marsala and stock, and boil the mixture down until it is a third of its original volume. Arrange the escalopes on plates and serve with the Marsala sauce.

Ossobuco
veal shanks in tomato and wine sauce

Serves 4

4 veal cutlets, bone in
2 tbsp flour
2 tbsp olive oil
2 onions
1 garlic clove
1 carrot
½ stick celery
200 g tomato passata
200 ml dry red wine
approx. 500 ml beef stock
½ bay leaf
4 tbsp freshly chopped herbs
salt
pepper

Preparation time: 20 minutes
(plus cooking time)
Per serving approx. 263 kcal/
1103 kJ
33 g P, 9 g F, 7 g CH

1 Coat the cutlets in flour and brown thoroughly in hot olive oil in a casserole dish, then remove from the dish.

2 Peel and finely chop the onions and garlic. Wash the carrot and celery, and cut into small pieces. Put the vegetables in a pan with the onions and garlic, and sauté for 3 minutes. Add the tomatoes and pour in the wine. Bring to a boil.

3 Lay the cutlets in the sauce and pour over the stock until everything is completely covered.

4 Add the bay leaf and half of the herbs. Cover the casserole dish with a lid and braise the meat for approx. an hour. After 30 minutes, turn the meat and season.

5 After an hour, remove the bay leaf and stir in the rest of the herbs. If the sauce is too thick, dilute it with a little wine, stock or water. Serve the ossobuco in its sauce.

Red meat and poultry

Saltimbocca
alla Romana

Serves 4

8 thin veal escalopes
(500 g in total)

1 tbsp flour

salt

black pepper

8 sage leaves

8 slices wafer-thin Parma
ham

2 tbsp olive oil

2 tbsp butter

125 ml white wine

Preparation time: 15 minutes
(plus cooking time)
Per serving approx. 260 kcal/
1090 kJ
27 g P, 13 g F, 2 g CH

1 Beat the escalopes flat between 2 layers of cling-film using a meat mallet or rolling pin. Mix the flour with salt and pepper, and lightly coat the escalopes.

2 Wash the sage leaves and pat dry with kitchen towel. Place a sage leaf and a slice of ham on each escalope. Secure both to the escalope with a wooden skewer or toothpick.

3 Heat the oil and butter in a pan and fry the escalopes for 2 to 3 minutes on each side. Cover with aluminium foil and keep warm in the oven at 50 °C. Deglaze the pan with the wine and bring to a rolling boil. Season with salt and pepper.

4 Serve the saltimbocca on pre-warmed plates. Pasta drizzled with the sauce makes a great accompaniment, along with a colourful leafy salad.

Kofte
Turkish meatballs

Serves 4

350 g bulgur wheat
1 large onion
3 garlic cloves
1 tsp vegetable stock
1 tbsp paprika paste
1–2 tbsp paprika powder
350 g minced beef
1 bunch flat-leaf parsley
olive oil for frying
chilli flakes for sprinkling
salad to serve (optional)

Preparation time: 15 minutes
(plus soaking time)
Per serving 478 kcal/2006 kJ
27 g P, 13 g F, 63 g CH

1 Wash the bulgur wheat, then leave to soak in a little water for 3 hours. Peel and finely chop the onion. Peel and crush the garlic cloves.

2 Mix the bulgur wheat, onion, garlic, stock, paprika paste and paprika powder thoroughly together in a bowl, and knead until the mixture is smooth.

3 Add the minced beef and mix everything well until it has a smooth, dough-like consistency.

4 Wash the parsley, shake dry and chop. Stir the parsley into the meatball mixture then shape into meatballs. Heat the oil in a pan and fry the kofte all over in batches. Serve sprinkled with the chilli flakes, with salad on the side.

Lamb kebabs
with yoghurt

Serves 4

675 g lamb shoulder
1 large onion
2 garlic cloves
juice of 1 lemon
5 tbsp olive oil
1 tsp ground cumin
2 tsp paprika powder
salt
pepper
675 g tomatoes
pinch of sugar
1 tsp tomato purée
30 g pine nuts
2 thin flatbreads
350 ml whole milk yoghurt
½ bunch parsley, chopped

Preparation time: 55 minutes
Per serving approx. 543 kcal/
2279 kJ
56 g P, 29 g F, 13 g CH

1 Wash and dry the meat and cut into cubes. Peel and grate the onion, and crush the garlic cloves.

2 Mix the onion and garlic with the lemon juice, 2 tablespoons of oil, the cumin, 1 teaspoon of paprika powder, salt and pepper, and spread over the meat. Marinate the meat for a minimum of 4 hours, turning occasionally.

3 To make the sauce, score crosses into the tomatoes, scald with boiling water, remove the skins, seeds and core, and chop the flesh. Heat 1 tablespoon of olive oil and simmer the tomatoes for approx. 10 minutes with the sugar, tomato purée, salt and pepper.

4 Heat the grill to its highest setting. Remove the meat from the marinade and thread onto metal skewers. Grill the kebabs on each side for 5 minutes, basting with the marinade several times. Toast the pine nuts, and halve and toast the flatbreads.

5 Place the flatbreads on a platter, spread with the tomato sauce and arrange the kebabs on top. Top with the yoghurt and pine nuts. Warm the rest of the oil, mix with the rest of the paprika powder and pour over the kebabs. Serve garnished with parsley.

Red meat and poultry

Chicken

in lemon and saffron sauce

Serves 4

4 chicken legs

salt

pepper

2 tbsp oil

1 Spanish onion

2 untreated lemons

a few saffron threads

250 ml vegetable stock

½ bunch chopped lemon
  balm

Preparation time: 15 minutes
(plus frying and cooking time)
Per serving approx. 310 kcal/
1302 kJ
28 g P, 19 g F, 6 g CH

1 Rub the chicken legs with salt and pepper, and fry in the hot oil until they are brown all over. Remove from the pan.

2 Peel the onion, cut into rings, and fry until translucent in the cooking fat. Return the chicken legs to the pan.

3 Wash the lemons in hot water and dry. Squeeze one of the lemons and add the juice to the meat along with the saffron and stock. Cut the second lemon into quarters and add to the pan.

4 Cover the pan and leave everything to braise for approx. 45 minutes. Serve with the chopped lemon balm. Rice makes a good accompaniment for this dish.

Meatballs
with dates and almonds

Serves 4

150 g cooked rice
500 g minced pork
1 egg
20 g toasted almond flakes
salt
pepper
125 g dates
½ lemon
1 tbsp mustard
4 tbsp breadcrumbs
olive oil for frying
4 onions
100 ml white wine
100 ml strong meat stock
2 bay leaves

Preparation time: 25 minutes
(plus cooking time)
Per serving approx. 655 kcal/
2751 kJ
29 g P, 31 g F, 60 g CH

1 Mix the rice with the minced pork, egg and almond flakes, and add salt and pepper. Pit the dates, cut into small pieces and place in a bowl with the meat mixture. Wash and dry the lemon halves, grate the zest and add to the other ingredients along with the mustard.

2 Working with damp hands, form small meatballs. Roll the meatballs in the breadcrumbs and fry in the oil. Peel and finely chop the onions. Fry until translucent in a little oil, then pour in the wine and stock. Add the bay leaves. Bring everything to a boil and leave to simmer for approx. 10 minutes.

3 Place the meatballs in the broth and leave to stand for 15 minutes. Leave the meatballs to cool in the broth, then serve with bread.

Pork loin
with chorizo

Serves 4

600 g Pork tenderloin

6 garlic cloves

1 sprig oregano

1 bay leaf

salt

pepper

2 small chorizo sausages
  (approx. 200 g)

1 tsp paprika

50 g pork dripping

Preparation time: 15 minutes
(plus cooking and frying time)
Per serving approx. 595 kcal/
2499 kJ
53 g P, 42 g F, 3 g CH

1 Cut the pork tenderloin into bite-sized pieces. Peel and roughly chop the garlic.

2 Wash the oregano, shake dry and tear the leaves from their stalks. Chop finely.

3 Place the cubes of pork in a stew pot. Add the garlic, oregano, bay leaf and a little salt and pepper. Pour in approx. 175 ml water, then cover and leave to simmer for 10–15 minutes.

4 Cut the chorizo into thin slices and add to the meat. Mix in the paprika and the pork dripping and simmer everything a little longer, uncovered, until the meat is tender and the water has boiled off.

5 Finally, fry the meat thoroughly in the dripping and serve immediately.

Spicy pork kebabs
African-style

Serves 4

150 ml olive oil
1 tsp chopped thyme
2 tbsp chopped parsley
1 tsp chilli powder
2 tsp ground cumin
1 tsp mild paprika
pepper
700 g pork
12–16 wooden skewers

Preparation time: 30 minutes
(plus marinating and cooking
time)
Per serving approx. 633 kcal/
2657 kJ
37 g P, 54 g F, 3 g CH

1 Put the olive oil in a bowl and add the thyme and parsley.

2 Add the chilli powder along with the ground cumin, paprika and a little pepper. Mix everything together thoroughly.

3 Cut the pork into 2 cm x 2 cm cubes. Add the pork cubes to the spice mixture and stir. Cover and leave to marinate overnight in the fridge.

4 The next day, remove the meat from the marinade and thread onto the soaked wooden skewers. Pre-heat the grill. Place the marinade in a pot and bring to a boil.

5 Roast the kebabs on the grill for approx. 5–10 minutes, basting regularly with the marinade.

Chicken legs
Andalusian-style

Serves 4

1 onion

4 garlic cloves

2 tbsp raisins

200 ml dry sherry

1 kg chicken legs

salt

black pepper

½ tsp ground cumin

4 tbsp olive oil

1 cinnamon stick

50 g sliced almonds

pinch of ground cinnamon
(optional)

Preparation time: 15 minutes
(plus cooking time)
Per serving approx. 560 kcal/
2340 kJ
37 g P, 38 g F, 4 g CH

1 Peel and finely chop the onion and garlic. Place the raisins in a bowl, pour over 3 tablespoons of sherry and leave to stand for 10 minutes. Wash the chicken legs in cold water and pat dry. Rub salt, pepper and cumin into the skin.

2 Heat the olive oil in a casserole dish and sweat the onion with the garlic. Add the chicken legs and brown on all sides. Deglaze the dish with the sherry, then break the cinnamon stick in half and drop into in the cooking liquid. Cover and simmer over a low heat for approx. 45 minutes.

3 10 minutes before the cooking time is up, add the raisins and almond flakes to the chicken legs, mix well and add salt, pepper, cumin and cinnamon to taste. Remove the cinnamon stick before serving. Place the chicken legs on plates and decorate with flaked almonds and the crumbled cinnamon stick. This dish works well with rice.

Duck legs
in a fruity sauce

Serves 4

4–6 duck legs

salt

pepper

1 onion

4 garlic cloves

2 carrots

1 orange

1 tbsp clarified butter

1 tsp flour

1 bay leaf

1 dried chilli

500 ml dry white wine

175 g green olives

sugar

1 tbsp wine vinegar

Preparation time: 25 minutes
(plus roasting time)
Per serving approx. 558 kcal/
2342 kJ
28 g P, 40 g F, 13 g CH

1 Pre-heat the oven to 225 °C (Gas Mark 7, fan oven 200 °C). Rub salt and pepper into the duck legs. Peel and finely chop the onion and garlic. Peel and slice the carrots. Wash the orange with hot water, dry and cut into slices.

2 Sear the duck legs in the hot clarified butter. Add the onion, garlic and carrot and fry briefly. Sprinkle everything with flour. Add the bay leaf, chilli and orange slices. Roast in the pre-heated oven at 200 °C (Gas Mark 6, fan oven 180 °C) for approx. 20 minutes until crispy. Pour in the wine and cook for another 20 minutes.

3 Pit and slice the olives. Remove the bay leaf, chilli and orange slices from the casserole dish. Boil the sauce down to 1/3 of its original volume and warm the olives in the sauce. Season with salt, pepper, sugar and vinegar. Serve the duck legs with the sauce.

Moussaka
aubergine and lamb bake

Serves 4

3 aubergines

salt

1 onion

1 garlic clove

125 ml olive oil

400 g minced lamb

pepper

400 g chopped tinned
tomatoes

2 tbsp tomato purée

1/2 tsp ground cinnamon

2 tbsp freshly chopped
parsley

2 tsp finely chopped mint

3 tbsp butter, plus extra for
greasing

3 tbsp flour

300 ml milk

75 g Alpine cheese

Preparation time: 30 minutes
(plus cooking time)
Per serving approx. 570 kcal/
2386 kJ
41 g P, 39 g F, 15 g CH

1 Cut the aubergines into ½ cm thick slices, sprinkle with salt and leave to stand for 1 hour. Chop the onion and garlic clove finely and fry thoroughly in 2 tablespoons of oil along with the minced lamb. Season with salt and pepper. Add the tomatoes with their juice to the meat, stir in the tomato purée, fold in the herbs and spices, then remove the pan from the heat.

2 Rinse the aubergine slices, pat dry and fry on both sides in lots of oil in batches. Place alternating layers of aubergine slices and lamb sauce in a greased casserole dish. Finish with a layer of aubergine slices.

3 Make a roux out of melted butter and flour, add milk and boil down to form a smooth sauce. Season and pour over the contents of the casserole dish. Scatter over the grated cheese and bake for approx. 45 minutes in the oven at 220 °C (Gas Mark 7, fan oven 200 °C).

Gyros

with cucumber dip

Serves 4

600 g pork escalopes

3 tbsp gyro spice

3 tbsp oil

1 cucumber

2 onions

1 garlic clove

1 bunch dill

1 tbsp lemon juice

300 g natural yoghurt

salt

pepper

a little chilli powder

Preparation time: 20 minutes
(plus marinating and frying time)
Per serving approx. 328 kcal/
1378 kJ
37 g P, 15 g F, 9 g CH

1 Wash the escalopes, pat dry and cut into thin strips. Mix with the gyro spice and oil in a bowl and marinate for approx. 45 minutes.

2 Wash, peel, halve and deseed the cucumber and cut into fine slices. Peel and finely chop the onions and garlic clove. Wash the dill, shake dry and chop finely. Place the cucumber, onion, garlic and dill in a bowl and mix in the lemon juice. Stir in the yoghurt and season with salt, pepper and chilli powder.

3 Brown the meat thoroughly on all sides in a hot pan and leave to cook over a gentle heat for approx. another 10 minutes. Serve with the cucumber dip and rice.

Cevapcici
with tzatziki

Serves 4

½ cucumber
salt
4 garlic cloves
250 g curd cheese
150 g yoghurt
pepper
1 tbsp finely chopped parsley
600 g minced beef
paprika
1 onion
1 red pepper
1 green pepper
3 tbsp olive oil

Preparation time: 20 minutes
(plus standing and cooling time)
Per serving approx. 432 kcal/
1814 kJ
40 g P, 26 g F, 8 g CH

1 Wash, peel and finely grate the cucumber. Sprinkle with a little salt and leave to stand for 15 minutes. Peel one of the garlic cloves and chop finely. Squeeze out the grated cucumber and mix with the garlic, curd cheese and yoghurt in a bowl. Season with salt, pepper and parsley.

2 Peel and finely chop the rest of the garlic cloves and knead with the minced beef, salt, pepper and paprika to form a firm mixture. Shape this into finger-long, 2 cm thick sausages and leave on a plate in the fridge for approx. 30 minutes.

3 Peel and chop the onion. Wash and deseed the peppers and slice into narrow strips. Heat the oil in a pan and fry the cevapcici on all sides for approx. 5 minutes, turning frequently. Serve with the tzatziki, pepper strips and chopped onion.

Coq au vin
the French national dish

Serves 4

1 ready-to-cook chicken
(approx. 1.3 kg)

salt

black pepper

1 tsp sweet paprika

3 shallots

2 garlic cloves

3 carrots

4 tomatoes

300 g small mushrooms

2 tbsp butter

80 g chopped streaky bacon

50 ml Cognac

1 tbsp flour

600 ml dry red wine

½ bunch flat-leaf
parsley, finely chopped

Preparation time: 20 minutes
(plus cooking time)
Per serving approx. 700 kcal/
2930 kJ
48 g P, 41 g F, 15 g CH

1 Rinse the chicken with cold water and pat dry. Divide into 6 to 8 portions using poultry scissors. Rub the inside and outside with salt, pepper and a little paprika.

2 Peel and very finely chop the shallots and garlic. Wash and peel the carrots. Cut into strips lengthways, and then dice. Score crosses into the tomatoes, blanch in boiling water, refresh in cold water, then skin with a small kitchen knife, cut into quarters, deseed and remove the cores. Cut the flesh into cubes. Rub the mushrooms clean with kitchen paper.

3 Melt the butter in a stew pot, add the chopped bacon and fry. Add the mushrooms and fry on all sides, the remove the bacon and mushrooms from the pot and set to one side.

4 Place the chicken pieces in the pot and brown on all sides. Pour in the Cognac and set fire to it with a match. Add the vegetables once the flame has gone out, coat with flour and deglaze with red wine. Cover the pot and braise over a low heat for an hour.

5 In the last 5 minutes of cooking, return the mushrooms and fried bacon to the coq au vin to warm through. Season everything with salt, pepper and paprika and scatter over the parsley. Serve the coq au vin with fresh French bread or potato dumplings.

Lamb ragù
with mushrooms

Serves 4

1 kg boneless leg of lamb

500 g button mushrooms

200 g onions

3 tbsp olive oil

125 ml dry white wine

salt

pepper

1 tbsp freshly chopped
  rosemary

2 tbsp Marsala

Preparation time: 25 minutes
(plus braising and cooking time)
Per serving approx. 452 kcal/
1900 kJ
56 g P, 13 g F, 5 g CH

1 Cut the lamb into cubes. Clean the mushrooms by rubbing them with a damp thumb. Peel the onions and chop roughly.

2 Pre-heat the oven to 190 °C (Gas Mark 5, fan oven 170 °C). Heat the olive oil in a pot and brown the meat thoroughly. Sauté the onions in the pot. Add the mushrooms and wine, and fill with enough water to completely cover the meat. Season with salt, pepper and rosemary.

3 Cover the pot and cook the ragù in the oven for approx. an hour, until the meat is completely tender. Add Marsala to taste.

Swordfish
in vegetable and saffron sauce

Serves 4

4 swordfish steaks

salt

pepper

juice of 2 lemons

120 g flour

6 tbsp olive oil

1 onion

2 carrots

100 g celeriac

1 leek

200 ml dry white wine

150 ml cream

pinch of ground saffron

2 tbsp freshly chopped dill

Preparation time: 20 minutes
Per serving approx. 555 kcal/
2324 kJ
37 g P, 26 g F, 33 g CH

1 Add salt and pepper to the swordfish steaks and marinate in the lemon juice. Coat in 100 g of flour and fry for approx. 3 minutes on each side in hot olive oil. Remove from the pan and keep warm.

2 Peel and dice the onion, carrots and celeriac. Slice the leek into rings.

3 Sauté the vegetables in the cooking fat for 5 minutes. Sprinkle over the rest of the flour. Pour in the white wine and cream, add the saffron and let the sauce boil down a little. Season with salt and pepper, and serve with the cooked swordfish steaks. Scatter over the chopped dill.

Oven-baked sea bream
with herbs

Serves 4

1 large, ready-to-cook sea
   bass
4 bay leaves
1 bunch parsley
1 sprig thyme
a few tarragon leaves
a few sprigs basil
butter for greasing
135 ml olive oil
salt
pepper
flour
fresh herbs for garnishing

Preparation time: 30 minutes
(plus standing and roasting time)
Per serving approx. 475 kcal/
1989 kJ
32 g P, 38 g F, 3 g CH

1 Wash the fish and pat dry thoroughly. Put the bay leaves and ⅓ of the washed and dried herbs in a greased baking dish, stuff the fish with some of the herbs, place it in the baking dish and cover with the rest of the herbs. Pour over 45 ml of olive oil and leave to stand in a cool place for approx. 1 hour. Remove the fish from the baking dish and pat dry.

2 Season the fish with salt and pepper, then coat in flour.

3 Heat the rest of the olive oil in another baking dish and flash-fry the fish on both sides. Place in the oven and roast for approx. 35–40 minutes at 200 °C (Gas Mark 6, fan oven 180 °C), basting several times with the herb oil. The fish is ready when the dorsal fin can be pulled out easily. Serve garnished with fresh herbs.

Squid stew
with olives

Serves 4

600 g ready-to-cook squid
  with tentacles

2 onions

1 garlic clove

4 tbsp olive oil

400 g tomato passata

100 g pitted green olives

2 tbsp capers

500 ml fish stock

200 ml white wine

salt

pepper

pinch of sugar

4 tomatoes

1 bunch tarragon

Preparation time: 30 minutes
(plus cooking time)
Per serving approx. 310 kcal/
1298 kJ
29 g P, 12 g F, 13 g CH

1 Wash the squid and cut into small pieces. Peel and chop the onions and garlic. Sauté the squid in hot olive oil, then add the onion and garlic and fry. Stir in the tomato passata. Chop and add the olives and capers, pour in the stock and wine, and season with salt, pepper and sugar. Cover and leave to simmer for approx. 1 hour.

2 Skin, deseed and dice the fresh tomatoes and chop the tarragon. Stir into the sauce, heat through and serve with bread.

Stuffed mussels
with tomatoes

Serves 4

1.5 kg mussels

5 eggs

250 g breadcrumbs

125 g freshly grated
Pecorino

3 tbsp freshly chopped
parsley

1 garlic clove

3 tbsp olive oil

400 g tomato passata

salt

pepper

1 tbsp freshly chopped
oregano

Preparation time: 30 minutes
(plus baking and cooking time)
Per serving approx. 768 kcal/
3224 kJ
60 g P, 30 g F, 64 g CH

1 Wash the mussels thoroughly under running water and discard any that are open. Pre-heat the oven to 200 °C (Gas Mark 6, fan oven 180 °C). Bring water to a boil in a large pot and cook the mussels for approx. 5 minutes until they open. Throw away any that do not open. Drain the mussels and leave to dry.

2 Whisk the eggs and mix with the breadcrumbs and cheese. Fold in the parsley and beat until creamy. Place the opened mussels on a baking tray and divide the egg mixture between them. Carefully close the mussel shells and bake the mussels in the oven for approx. 15 minutes.

3 Peel and finely chop the garlic for the sauce. Heat the oil in a pot and fry the garlic. Add the tomatoes and simmer the mixture over a medium heat for approx. 10 minutes. Add salt, pepper and oregano to taste.

Mediterranean
fish skewers

Serves 4

40 g cod fillet

8 shelled tiger prawns

1 courgette

12 cherry tomatoes

8 wooden skewers

1 garlic clove

4 tbsp olive oil

salt

pepper

1 tsp Italian mixed herbs

Preparation time: 15 minutes
(plus grilling time)
Per serving approx. 236 kcal/
991 kJ
38 g P, 7 g F, 3 g CH

1 Wash the fish fillets, pat dry and cut into bite-sized pieces. Remove any tendons from the prawns. Wash the courgette and cut into 1 cm-thick slices. Thread the ingredients onto the wooden skewers together with the cherry tomatoes.

2 Peel and crush the garlic clove. Make a marinade out of garlic, olive oil, salt, pepper and the Italian herbs, and brush it over the fish skewers.

3 Place the skewers on a baking tray covered in aluminium foil and grill for approx. 8 minutes under a grill heated to 250 °C (Gas Mark 10). Turn the skewers several times and baste occasionally with the marinade.

Fish
and almond tagine

Serves 4

1 onion
2 garlic cloves
100 ml olive oil
1 tbsp paprika
1 tsp turmeric
1 tsp cumin
salt
pepper
approx. 750 g tinned
   tomatoes
750 g firm white fish fillets
2 lemons
750 g leafy spinach
120 g peeled almonds

Preparation time: 20 minutes
(plus cooking time)
Per serving approx. 760 kcal/
3192 kJ
51 g P, 51 g F, 22 g CH

1 Peel and chop the onion and garlic and fry in hot oil. Stir in the paprika, turmeric, cumin, salt and pepper.

2 Add the tomatoes and 150 ml water, then leave to boil down for 15 minutes. Pre-heat the oven to 180 °C (Gas Mark 4, fan oven 160 °C).

3 Wash and dry the fish, and cut into large cubes. Wash the lemons and cut into quarters. Wash the spinach and slice finely.

4 Stir everything into the sauce. Cover the pot and bake in the oven for approx. 30 minutes. Season to taste, scatter over the almonds and serve.

Prawn
tagine

Serves 4

20 prawns

1 onion

1 garlic clove

150 ml olive oil

750 g tomatoes

1 tsp salt

1 tsp white pepper

¼ tsp sugar

750 g fennel

3 tbsp freshly chopped dill

3 tbsp freshly chopped flat-
leaf parsley

Preparation time: 50 minutes
Per serving approx. 765 kcal/
3213 kJ
108 g P, 28 g F, 17 g CH

1 Peel the prawns and remove the heads and veins. Wash thoroughly and pat dry. Peel and chop the onion and garlic. Heat 50 ml of olive oil in a pot and fry the onion and garlic for 5 minutes.

2 Score crosses into the tomatoes, blanch in hot water, skin, deseed, remove the cores and cut into cubes. Add the tomatoes, salt, pepper and sugar to the onion and simmer, stirring, for 10 minutes until the sauce has thickened. Set to one side.

3 Wash the fennel, trim the bulb and cut into rings. Bring a little water to a boil and blanch the fennel for approx. 5 minutes.

4 Heat 50 ml of oil in a pan and sauté the fennel until golden brown. Meanwhile, heat the rest of the oil in a second pan and fry the prawns on all sides for approx. 4 minutes.

5 Warm through the tomato sauce briefly and spoon onto a platter or into a tagine dish. Place the prawns and fennel on top. Scatter with dill and parsley, and serve.

Bulgur-stuffed
gilt-head sea bream

Serves 4

60 g bulgur wheat

4 shallots

1 stick celery

3 garlic cloves

vegetable oil

½ bunch chopped parsley

1 tbsp freshly chopped dill

½ tsp salt

freshly ground pepper

4 ready-to-cook gilt-head
  sea bream

1 lime, cut into quarters

Preparation time: 30 minutes
(plus soaking and cooking time)
Per serving approx. 367 kcal/
1536 kJ
50 g P, 13 g F, 10 g CH

1 Soak the bulgur wheat in approx. 100 ml of boiling water and leave to stand for 20 minutes, until the water has been absorbed.

2 Pre-heat the oven to 180 °C (Gas Mark 4, fan oven 160 °C). Peel and chop the shallots. Wash and chop the celery. Peel and slice the garlic.

3 Heat a little vegetable oil in a pan and fry the vegetables and the garlic over a medium heat for approx. 5 minutes, until the chopped shallots are translucent. Remove the pan from the stove and stir in the bulgur wheat, parsley, dill, salt and pepper.

4 Wash the sea bream thoroughly and rub dry. Stuff each fish with a quarter of the bulgur mixture. Place the fish on a baking tray covered with baking parchment and bake for approx. 30 minutes. The fish is ready when it can be crushed with a fork.

5 Remove the skins from the fish and sprinkle with ground pepper. Serve garnished with the lime quarters.

Pepper-stuffed sardines

Serves 4

2 red peppers
125 g butter
1 kg fresh sardines
sea salt
4 tbsp olive oil
2 tbsp breadcrumbs

Preparation time: 30 minutes
(plus cooking time)
Per serving approx. 570 kcal/
2394 kJ
50 g P, 39 g F, 6 g CH

1 Wash and halve the peppers and cut into thin strips.

2 Melt 80 g butter in a pan and fry the pepper strips gently until they are soft.

3 Clean the sardines and carefully remove the spines and guts. Wash the fish carefully and leave to dry.

4 Pre-heat the oven to 180 °C (Gas Mark 4, fan oven 160 °C). Sprinkle with sea salt, stuff with some of the pepper strips and press together firmly.

5 Pack the sardines tightly in an ovenproof dish, place the rest of the pepper strips on top and pour over the olive oil.

6 Sprinkle the breadcrumbs. Dab the rest of the butter on top and bake in the oven for approx. 15–20 minutes.

Galician squid
with king prawns

Serves 4

1 medium waxy potatoes
salt
300 g squid
175 g king prawns
3–5 tbsp olive oil
2 garlic cloves
1 tomato
pepper

Preparation time: 30 minutes
Per serving approx. 180 kcal/
757 kJ
22 g P, 5 g F, 10 g CH

1 Peel and wash the potatoes, cook in salted water for approx. 20 minutes, leave to cool a little, then cut into slices and place in a bowl. Wash the squid and slice into thin rings.

2 Peel and devein the prawns. Wash and leave to dry. Sprinkle with salt. Heat 2 tablespoons of oil, peel the garlic and sauté gently in the hot oil with the prawns and squid rings until the prawns are pink. Add to the bowl with the potatoes.

3 Scald the tomato with boiling water for 30 seconds, then skin and cut in half, remove the core and seeds, and dice finely. Scatter the tomato pieces over the ingredients in the bowl and mix everything carefully together.

4 Heat the rest of the olive oil until very hot and pour over the ingredients. Sprinkle with salt and pepper, mix together, arrange in bowls and serve with bread.

Baked prawns
with saffron mayonnaise

Serves 4

500 g ready-to-cook prawns

2 garlic cloves

75 ml olive oil

2 tbsp lemon juice

salt

2 egg yolks

pinch of ground saffron

approx. 200 ml sunflower oil

pepper

Preparation time: 15 minutes
(plus cooking time)
Per serving approx. 560 kcal/
2352 kJ
28 g P, 50 g F, 3 g CH

1 Pre-heat the oven to 175 °C (Gas Mark 3, fan oven 150 °C). Peel the prawns, but do not remove the tails. Wash and dry the prawns. Peel and finely chop the garlic.

2 Mix the olive oil, garlic, 1 tablespoon of lemon juice and salt together well. Add the prawns and mix thoroughly. Finally, put everything in a *cazuela* (cast-iron or stainless steel pot). Bake in the oven for approx. 20 minutes.

3 While the prawns are cooking, mix the egg yolks thoroughly with the ground saffron, salt and 1 tablespoon of lemon juice. Stir in the sunflower oil drop by drop to begin with, then in a thin stream. Season with salt and pepper. Serve the baked prawns with the saffron mayonnaise and toasted bread.

Mussels
with chilli and vegetables

Serves 4

5 onions
60 g ham
1 small red jalapeño pepper
2 tbsp olive oil
1 tbsp medium sherry
60 small ready-to-cook
  Venus mussels

Preparation time: 30 minutes
(plus cooking time)
Per serving approx. 170 kcal/
710 kJ
21 g P, 4 g F, 13 g CH

1 Peel the onions and slice into very thin rings. Cut the ham into tiny cubes. Wash, halve and finely dice the jalapeño.

2 Heat the olive oil, add the onions, cover and fry for 10 minutes until they are translucent.

3 Stir in the ham and jalapeño, pour in the sherry and add the mussels.

4 Place the lid on the pan and simmer for a few minutes over a low heat until the mussels open.

5 Remove the mussels, discard any that have not opened, and put the rest of the mussels back in the broth. Serve the mussels with their broth.

Salads and vegetables

Greek salad
a rustic mix

Serves 4

1 cucumber
2 yellow peppers
500 g tomatoes
2 spring onions
120 g black olives
200 g feta cheese
½ bunch flat-leaf parsley
6 sprigs thyme
1 garlic clove
4 tbsp white wine vinegar
6 tbsp olive oil
salt
black pepper

Preparation time: 30 minutes
Per serving approx. 420 kcal/
1760 kJ
12 g P, 36 g F, 12 g CH

1 Wash and peel the cucumber and cut in half lengthways. Cut into ½ cm thick pieces. Wash and halve the peppers, remove the membranes and seeds, and cut into cubes. Wash and halve the tomatoes, remove the cores and cut into eighths.

2 Wash the spring onions, remove the roots and the withered green outer parts and slice into very thin rings. Drain the olives and crumble the feta using your hands. Wash the parsley and pat dry. Tear the leaves from their stalks and chop finely. Mix all of the prepared ingredients together in a large salad bowl.

3 To make the dressing, wash the thyme and pat dry. Strip the leaves from their stalks. Peel the garlic and chop very finely using a large kitchen knife. Mix together the vinegar, olive oil, thyme and garlic. Season with salt and pepper and add to the salad mixture. Pitta bread makes a good accompaniment.

Salade niçoise
with artichokes

Serves 4

4 eggs
600 g tomatoes
1 cucumber
2 yellow peppers
4 spring onions
1 garlic clove
8 preserved artichokes
140 g canned tuna
8 anchovy fillets
1 sprig lemon thyme
2 sprigs basil
4 tbsp olive oil
2 tbsp red wine vinegar
salt
black pepper
80 g black olives
1 tbsp capers (from a jar)

Preparation time: 50 minutes
(plus cooking time)
Per serving approx. 430 kcal/
1800 kJ
21 g P, 30 g F, 15 g CH

1 Hard-boil the eggs, plunge in cold water, peel and then leave to cool. Cut into slices.

2 Wash the vegetables and pat dry. Halve the tomatoes, remove the stalks and cut into eighths. Peel the cucumber using a potato peeler and slice thinly. Halve the peppers and remove the cores, membranes and seeds. Cut the flesh into narrow strips. Wash the spring onions, remove the roots and the withered outer green parts and slice into very thin rings. Peel the garlic and chop finely with a large knife.

3 Remove the artichokes from the jar, drain well and cut in half. Drain the tuna and flake with a fork. Rinse the anchovy fillets with cold water, pat dry with kitchen paper and cut in half.

4 Wash the herbs and pat dry. Tear the thyme leaves from their stems. Do the same with the basil and chop finely.

5 Mix the oil with the red wine vinegar to make a marinade. Season with salt and pepper.

6 Arrange the salad on 4 large plates, then spoon the herbs, olives and capers over the top and drizzle with the marinade.

Spinach salad
with yoghurt

Serves 4

1 kg leafy spinach

4 garlic cloves

6 tbsp olive oil

salt

black pepper

200 g full milk yoghurt

juice of ½ lemon

Preparation time: 25 minutes
Per serving approx. 243 kcal/
1020 kJ
8 g P, 21 g F, 5 g CH

1 Make sure that all of the spinach leaves are fresh, then wash and leave to dry. Peel and crush the garlic.

2 Heat 3 tablespoons of oil in a large pot and sauté the garlic. Add the spinach and wilt over a low heat. Sauté for another 4 minutes, then season with salt and pepper.

3 Mix the yoghurt with the lemon juice and the rest of the olive oil. Place the spinach in a bowl and mix in the yoghurt. This salad goes well with pitta bread.

Panzanella
Italian bread salad

Serves 4

150 g stale white bread

125 ml vegetable stock

1 onion

1 garlic clove

200 g tomatoes

200 g cucumber

1 bunch basil

2 tbsp white balsamic vinegar

4 tbsp olive oil

salt

pepper

2 tbsp freshly shaved Parmesan

Preparation time: 20 minutes
Per serving approx. 173 kcal/
724 kJ
5 g P, 7 g F, 22 g CH

1 Cut the bread into cubes and soak in the cold vegetable stock for 15 minutes. Peel and finely chop the onion and garlic. Skin, deseed and dice the tomatoes. Peel and dice the cucumber. Wash the basil, shake dry and slice, keeping back a few leaves for garnishing.

2 Make a dressing out of the white balsamic vinegar, oil, salt and pepper. Remove the bread from the stock. Mix with the other ingredients, pour over the dressing and sprinkle with Parmesan.

Courgettes
with tomatoes and basil

Serves 4

500 g tomatoes

500 g courgettes

2 garlic cloves

2 shallots

1 bunch basil

3 tbsp olive oil

1 tbsp pine nuts

salt

pepper

Preparation time: 30 minutes
Per serving approx. 94 kcal/394 kJ
4 g P, 5 g F, 7 g CH

1 Scald the tomatoes with hot water, skin, deseed and cut into cubes. Dice the courgettes. Peel and chop the garlic and shallots. Wash the basil, shake dry and chop.

2 Heat the oil and fry the shallots and garlic until translucent. Add the pine nuts, tomatoes and courgettes and fry, stirring often. Add the basil, season with salt and pepper and leave to stand for another 15 minutes. Toasted white bread makes a good accompaniment to this salad.

Stuffed tomatoes
with olives

Serves 4

8 medium-sized tomatoes
(or 4 large tomatoes)

1 onion

2 garlic cloves

4 tbsp olive oil

75 g black olives

1 tbsp capers

1 tbsp chopped sunflower
seeds

1 bunch basil

salt

pepper

4 tbsp breadcrumbs

30 g Parmesan

Preparation time: 20 minutes
(plus baking time)
Per serving approx. 202 kcal/
846 kJ
5 g P, 16 g F, 9 g CH

1 Cut the top of each of the tomatoes to form a lid, remove the seeds with a spoon. Cut the flesh removed from the middle and the lid into small dice. Chop the onion and garlic cloves and sauté in 1 tablespoon of olive oil. Add the flesh from the tomatoes, the pitted and chopped olives, the drained capers, the sunflower seeds and the chopped basil and fry for approx. 5 minutes. Add salt and pepper.

2 Fry the breadcrumbs in 1 tablespoon of oil, then stir in 1 tablespoon of grated Parmesan. Stir half of this mixture into the vegetables and stuff into the hollowed-out tomatoes.

3 Place the tomatoes in a greased baking tin, scatter over the rest of the breadcrumb mixture and the rest of the cheese and drizzle with 2 tablespoons of olive oil. Bake in the oven for approx. 25 minutes at 200 °C (Gas Mark 6, fan oven 180 °C).

Vegetable casserole
with potatoes

Serves 4

300 g tomatoes

2 green peppers

2 aubergines

500 g potatoes

5 tbsp olive oil

250 g mozzarella

200 ml dry white wine

200 ml vegetable stock

salt

pepper

2 tbsp breadcrumbs

freshly chopped thyme

1 bunch basil

Preparation time: 20 minutes
(plus cooking time)
Per serving approx. 413 kcal/
1729 kJ
18 g P, 20 g F, 30 g CH

1 Cut the tomatoes, peppers and aubergines into thin slices or strips. Peel and slice the potatoes.

2 Brush an ovenproof dish with olive oil. Arrange the vegetables in the dish in alternating layers.

3 Slice the mozzarella and lay over the top. Pour over the wine and stock. Season with salt and pepper. Mix the breadcrumbs with the thyme and scatter over the dish. Bake for approx. an hour in the oven at 200 °C (Gas Mark 6, fan oven 180 °C). Cut the basil into strips and scatter over the casserole before serving.

Vegetable frittata
with Parmesan

Serves 4

200 g carrots

3 shallots

400 g courgettes

1 tbsp olive oil

1 garlic clove

1 tbsp rosemary

80 g Parmesan

4 eggs

3 tbsp cream

salt

pepper

Preparation time: 25 minutes
(plus cooking time)
Per serving approx. 182 kcal/
764 kJ
11 g P, 12 g F, 5 g CH

1 Peel the carrots and shallots, wash the courgettes and grate all three vegetables. Heat the olive oil in a pan and sauté the vegetables for 2 minutes. Peel the garlic clove and crush it into the pan. Stir in the rosemary. Sauté everything for another minute.

2 Pre-heat the oven to 200 °C (Gas Mark 6, fan oven 180 °C). Grate 2 tablespoons of Parmesan. Mix the eggs with the cream and Parmesan, and season with salt and pepper.

3 Spoon the vegetables into a greased round baking dish, pour over the egg and cream mixture, and bake in the oven for approx. 20 minutes. Before serving cut into wedges and scatter over Parmesan shavings.

Braised artichokes
with fresh mint

Serves 4

8 young artichokes
 (approx. 600 g)

salt

pepper

2 garlic cloves

4 tbsp olive oil

125 ml dry white wine

1 tbsp lemon juice

fresh mint

Preparation time: 20 minutes
(plus braising and cooking time)
Per serving approx. 83 kcal/
352 kJ
4 g P, 3 g F, 6 g CH

1 Wash the artichokes, cut off the stalks and remove the outer leaves. Cut off the hard tips of the remaining leaves with scissors. Season the artichokes with salt and pepper.

2 Peel and finely chop the garlic. Heat the oil in a large pan and sauté the garlic for 2 minutes. Add the artichokes to the pan and cook over a medium heat for another 2 minutes until they are golden brown.

3 Pour in the wine, cover the pan and cook the artichokes for approx. 30 minutes, until they are tender and have a good colour. Add more wine if necessary.

4 Remove the artichokes from the pan and drizzle with lemon juice. Serve immediately with the fresh mint leaves and bread.

Aubergine and
mozzarella gratin

Serves 4

800 g medium-sized
  aubergines
salt
300 g mozzarella
½ bunch oregano
½ bunch basil
500 g tinned tomatoes
100 g flour
100 ml olive oil
50 g freshly grated
  Parmesan

Preparation time: 30 minutes
(plus cooking time)
Per serving approx. 445 kcal/
1869 kJ
25 g P, 26 g F, 27 g CH

1 Wash the aubergines, pat dry and cut lengthways into ½ cm thick slices. Place the slices in a bowl, sprinkle with salt and leave to stand for approx. 15 minutes.

2 Pre-heat the oven to 180 °C (Gas Mark 4, fan oven 160 °C). Cut the mozzarella into small cubes. Wash the herbs, shake dry, tear the leaves from their stalks and chop. Put the tomatoes in a bowl and purée using a stick blender. Mix the herbs into the tomato purée.

3 Take the aubergines out of the bowl, rinse and pat dry. Turn the slices in the flour to coat. Heat the olive oil in a pan and fry the slices on both sides until golden brown. Leave to dry on kitchen paper.

4 Grease a baking dish and place alternate layers of aubergine slices, tomato purée and mozzarella in it, finishing off with a layer of tomato purée. Scatter the Parmesan over the top. Bake in the oven for approx. 10 minutes.

Ratatouille
with dates

Serves 4

1 onion

1 red pepper

4 tomatoes

4 tbsp cold-pressed oil

1 sprig rosemary

4 garlic cloves

1 aubergine

2 small courgettes

100 g dates

2 tsp sweet paprika

salt

freshly ground black pepper

40 g toasted flaked almonds

Preparation time: 30 minutes
(plus roasting and baking time)
Per serving approx. 365 kcal/
1533 kJ
7 g P, 25 g F, 29 g CH

1 Pre-heat the oven to 190 °C (Gas Mark 5, fan oven 170 °C). Peel and finely chop the onion. Wash and halve the pepper, remove the core and seeds, and cut into small dice. Score crosses into the tomatoes, scald in boiling water, then skin them and chop the flesh into fine dice.

2 Heat half of the oil in a pot. Sauté the onions and pepper, then leave to simmer for 3 minutes until soft. Wash the rosemary and shake dry. Peel the garlic.

3 Add the tomatoes and rosemary, and crush the garlic into the pot. Stir once and set to one side. Wash the aubergine and courgettes, remove the stalks and chop into small dice.

4 Heat the rest of the oil in another pot and fry the chopped aubergine and courgette for 3–4 minutes until golden brown, then remove from the pot and leave to dry on kitchen paper.

5 Pit the dates, cut into small pieces and fold into the vegetable mixture along with the paprika and the chopped aubergine and courgettes. Cover and bake in the oven for approx. 30 minutes. Remove the rosemary, add salt and pepper and garnish with the toasted flaked almonds.

Potatoes
with sea salt and aioli

Serves 4

750 g small waxy potatoes
sea salt
3 garlic cloves
approx. 150 g mayonnaise
⅓ bunch parsley

Preparation time: 25 minutes
(plus cooking and baking time)
Per serving approx. 325 kcal/
1365 kJ
5 g P, 21 g F, 29 g CH

1 Scrub and wash the potatoes and place in a pot with generously salted water. Add salt until the potatoes float on the surface of the water. If they sink to the bottom, add more salt. Boil the potatoes for 15–20 minutes.

2 Meanwhile, to make the aioli, peel the garlic, crush and add to the mayonnaise. Wash the parsley, shake dry and chop finely, then add to the mayonnaise and stir.

3 Drain the potatoes, return them to the pot, sprinkle with sea salt and then put the pot back on the stove. Cook over a low heat, shaking the pot constantly, until the salt on the potatoes has crystallised.

4 As soon as the salt has crystallised, turn off the heat, cover the pot with a tea towel and leave to stand for 5 minutes. Serve the potatoes with the aioli.

Ratatouille
French vegetable stew

Serves 4

300 g aubergines
salt
500 g tomatoes
250 g courgettes
1 red pepper
1 green pepper
1 yellow pepper
2 onions
4 garlic cloves
½ bunch basil
4 tbsp olive oil
black pepper
1 sprig of rosemary
½ bunch thyme
½ bunch oregano

Preparation time: 30 minutes
(plus cooking time)
Per serving approx. 170 kcal/
710 kJ
5 g P, 11 g F, 12 g CH

1 Wash the aubergines, rub dry and remove the stalks. Halve lengthways and cut into ½ cm thick slices. Sprinkle with salt and leave to stand for approx. 10 minutes in order to get rid of any bitterness. Rinse with water, pat dry and cut into cubes.

2 Score crosses into the tomatoes, scald briefly with boiling water, then plunge in cold water, skin, cut into quarters, deseed and remove the cores. Cut into cubes. Wash the courgettes and cut into small dice. Wash and halve the peppers and cut the flesh into cubes. Peel and very finely chop the onions and garlic. Wash the basil and pat dry with kitchen paper. Chop the leaves finely with a large kitchen knife.

3 Heat the olive oil in a casserole dish. Fry the aubergine cubes in the oil at a high heat, then remove and set to one side. Do the same with the other vegetables. Leave the onions and garlic to last. Sweat them in the oil, then return the other vegetables to the dish. Season with salt and pepper, place the sprigs of herbs on top, cover and leave the ratatouille to braise over a low heat for approx. 25 minutes. Add a little water if necessary.

4 Serve the ratatouille as an accompaniment to roast meat, rice or French bread.

Pizzas and breads

Flatbreads
with stuffing

Serves 8

600 ml milk

20 g yeast

2 tbsp sugar

1 kg flour

200 ml sunflower oil

1 tsp salt

750 g minced meat or
   sheep's cheese

1 egg yolk

butter for spreading

Preparation time: 40 minutes
(plus standing time)
Per serving approx. 1800 kcal/
7560 kJ
69 g P, 86 g F, 187 g CH

1 Warm the milk, mix with the yeast and sugar, and leave to stand for 30 minutes. Stir in the flour, oil and salt to make a smooth dough, then leave to rest for 60 minutes.

2 Meanwhile, prepare the filling: season and fry the minced meat or cut the sheep's cheese into small pieces. Divide the dough into several portions and roll out into oval shapes.

3 Pre-heat the oven to 200 °C (Gas Mark 6, fan oven 180 °C). Place a tablespoon of filling in the middle of each piece of dough and fold the edges inwards so that the filling is completely covered.

4 Fill all of the pieces of dough in the same way. Brush the edges of the dough with whisked egg yolk, place the flatbreads on a baking tray and bake in the oven for 20 minutes until golden brown. Spread with butter and serve hot.

Turkish pizza
with minced lamb

Serves 4

350 g durum wheat flour

7 g dried yeast

1½ tsp salt

1 tsp sugar

1 red onion

1 mild red chilli

200 g minced lamb

1 tsp paprika

2 tsp paprika paste

oil for greasing

1 tsp sumac (Turkish spice)

juice of 1 lemon

Preparation time: 30 minutes
(plus resting time)
Per serving approx. 435 kcal/
1827 kJ
24 g P, 6 g F, 70 g CH

1 Mix the flour with 1 teaspoon of salt and 1 teaspoon of sugar. Make a well in the middle of the mixture and fill it with 200 ml of warm water. Mix everything thoroughly right away and add water until it forms a smooth dough.

2 Knead the dough well, then cover and set aside in a warm place for 35 minutes. Peel the onion, chop one half, and slice the other half. Wash, deseed and chop the chilli.

3 Mix the minced lamb with the chopped onion, chilli, paprika powder and paste, and the rest of the salt. Blend using a food processor in order to bring the mixture to a smooth consistency.

4 Pre-heat the oven to 220 °C (Gas Mark 7, fan oven 200 °C). Divide the dough into four equally sized pieces and roll out into ovals 0.5 cm thick. Grease two baking trays and lay the four ovals out on them.

5 Spoon the meat mixture onto the dough bases. Bake each tray for approx. 12 minutes, until the meat is cooked. As soon as they come out of the oven, sprinkle the pizzas with sumac, place onion rings on top, drizzle with lemon juice and roll up.

Focaccia
with olives

Makes 1 round pizza

275 g flour

½ tsp salt

1 tsp dried yeast

7 tbsp olive oil

12 large green olives

Preparation time: 20 minutes
(plus resting and baking time)
Per pizza approx. 520 kcal/2177 kJ
29 g P, 31 g F, 52 g CH

1 Make a yeast dough from the flour, salt, dried yeast, 175 ml of warm water and 2 tablespoons of olive oil. Knead the dough thoroughly and lay in a round pizza pan, greased with 1 tablespoon of oil. Press the dough until it is 2 cm thick. Cover and leave to prove for 30 minutes.

2 Halve and deseed the olives. Using your fingers, make small dents in the dough and insert the olives.

3 Salt the dough lightly, then drizzle over the remaining 4 tablespoons of olive oil. Bake the focaccia for 25 minutes in the oven at 200 °C (Gas Mark 6, fan oven 180 °C). Serve hot.

Pizza Bambino
with salami

Serves 4

450 g flour

1 packet dried yeast

pinch of sugar

½ tsp salt

5 tbsp olive oil

1 onion

1 tbsp butter

400 g chunky tinned
  tomatoes

salt

pepper

1 tbsp dried oregano

2 small courgettes

200 g button mushrooms

2 yellow peppers

100 g Italian sliced salami

flour for the worktop

butter for greasing

250 g mozzarella

100 g middle-aged Gouda

Preparation time: 40 minutes
(plus resting and baking time)
Per serving approx. 457 kcal/
1913 kJ
26 g P, 36 g F, 6 g CH

1 Place the flour, yeast and sugar in a bowl, slowly add salt, oil and 500 ml of lukewarm water, and work everything into a smooth dough. Cover and leave to prove in a warm place for approx. 1 hour.

2 Sauté the chopped onion in the warm butter. Deglaze with the juice from the tomatoes, then add the tomato chunks, season with salt, pepper and oregano, and leave the mixture to boil down a little. Slice the zucchini and mushrooms, and cut the peppers and salami into strips.

3 Knead the dough on a floured surface, then roll out onto a greased baking tray and leave to prove for another 10 minutes.

4 Spread the tomato sauce on the dough. Arrange the vegetables, mushrooms and salami strips on top, and season with salt, pepper and oregano. Slice the mozzarella and divide between the pizzas. Scatter with the grated Gouda. Bake in the oven at 220 °C (Gas Mark 7, fan oven 200 °C) for approx. 25 minutes.

Pizza contadina
with spinach and bacon

Makes 1 round pizza

250 g flour

25 g yeast

salt

6 tbsp olive oil

400 g tomatoes

4 onions

4 garlic cloves

pepper

½ tsp sugar

½ tsp dried oregano

½ tsp dried thyme

175 g pork belly

250 g spinach

150 g grated Parmesan

Preparation time: 30 minutes
(plus resting and baking time)
Per pizza approx. 853 kcal/
3571 kJl
25 g P, 61 g F, 53 g CH

1 Make a dough out of flour, yeast, 100 ml of luke-warm water, a pinch of salt and 4 tablespoons of olive oil. Leave to prove for 1 hour.

2 Skin, deseed and dice the tomatoes. Peel and chop 2 onions and 2 garlic cloves, and sauté in 1 tablespoon of hot olive oil. Add the tomatoes, season with salt, pepper, sugar, oregano and thyme, and boil down a little until it forms a smooth tomato sauce.

3 Roll out the dough and place in the oiled pizza pan, then spread with the tomato sauce.

4 Peel and dice the remaining onions and garlic. Dice the bacon. Fry until golden brown in a tablespoon of hot olive oil, then sauté the onions and garlic cloves in the fat. Remove from the heat.

5 Cut the spinach into strips and place on the dough, add the bacon and onion mixture on top, and scatter over the cheese. Bake the pizza in the oven at 200 °C (Gas Mark 6, fan oven 180 °C) for approx. 20 minutes.

Pizza Vesuvio
with Gorgonzola

Makes 1 round pizza

250 g flour

25 g fresh yeast

salt

5 tbsp olive oil

400 g tomatoes

2 onions

2 garlic cloves

pepper

½ tsp sugar

½ tsp dried oregano

50 g grated Pecorino

1 red pepper

50 g Gorgonzola

½ red chilli

2 tbsp herb oil

Preparation time: 30 minutes
(plus resting and baking time)
Per pizza approx. 453 kcal/1897 kJ
14 g P, 15 g F, 64 g CH

1 Make a yeast dough from the flour, yeast, 100 ml lukewarm water, a pinch of salt and 4 tablespoons of olive oil. Leave to prove for an hour.

2 Skin, deseed and dice the tomatoes. Peel and chop the onions and garlic, and sauté in 1 tablespoon of hot olive oil. Add the tomatoes, season with salt, pepper, sugar and oregano, and boil down a little until it is a smooth tomato sauce.

3 Roll out the dough and place in the oiled pizza pan, forming a crust around the edge. Spread with the tomato sauce. Scatter over 25 g Pecorino. Place the pepper strips on top. Cut the Gorgonzola into fine dice and chop the chilli finely. Place everything on top of the pizza. Scatter over the rest of the Pecorino and drizzle with the herb oil. Bake in the oven at 220 °C (Gas Mark 7, fan oven 200 °C) for approx. 20 minutes.

Potato pizza
with Parmesan

Makes 1 round pizza

250 g flour

25 g fresh yeast

salt

6 tbsp olive oil

400 g tomatoes

2 onions

2 garlic cloves

pepper

½ tsp sugar

½ tsp dried oregano

500 g potatoes

1 tsp freshly chopped
rosemary

75 g grated Parmesan

Preparation time: 35 minutes
(plus resting and baking time)
Per pizza approx. 345 kcal/1444 kJ
18 g P, 33 g F, 68 g CH

1 Make a yeast dough from the flour, yeast, 100 ml of lukewarm water, a pinch of salt and 4 tablespoons of olive oil. Leave to prove for an hour. Skin, deseed and dice the tomatoes. Peel and chop the onions and garlic, and sauté in 1 tablespoon of hot olive oil. Add the tomatoes, season with salt, pepper, sugar and oregano, and boil down until it is a smooth tomato sauce.

2 Roll out the dough and place in an oiled pizza pan. Pull the dough to form a crust and leave to prove. Spread with the tomato sauce. Peel the potatoes, cut into fine slices and place on the pizza. Sprinkle over salt, pepper, rosemary and Parmesan. Drizzle over the rest of the olive oil. Bake in the oven at 200 °C (Gas Mark 6, fan oven 180 °C) for approx. 35 minutes.

Desserts and sweet dishes

Amaretto parfait
with figs

Serves 4

3 eggs

125 g sugar

3 tbsp amaretto

300 ml whipped cream

seeds of ½ vanilla pod

4 figs

2 tbsp Cognac

Preparation time: 20 minutes
Per serving approx. 425 kcal/
1779 kJ
8 g P, 28 g F, 29 g CH

1 Separate one of the eggs. In a warm bain-marie, stir 2 eggs and the egg yolk from the separated egg with 90 g sugar until frothy. Slowly pour in the amaretto and stir the mixture for another 5 minutes.

2 Add the cream to the vanilla seeds and mix together with the egg froth. Pour into 4 pudding moulds and freeze for approx. 3 hours. Cut the figs into quarters and marinate with the Cognac and 35 g sugar in a bowl. Turn the parfait out onto dessert plates and serve with the marinated figs. A fruit sauce would make a good accompaniment.

Torta al limone
Italian lemon cake

Serves 4

12 large eggs

175 g sugar

1 sachet vanilla sugar

150 g chopped almonds

zest and juice of 4 untreated
  lemons

zest of 1 untreated orange

300 g wheat flour

½ tsp salt

butter for greasing

icing sugar

Preparation time: 20 minutes
(plus baking time)
Per serving approx. 465 kcal/
1947 kJ
19 g P, 21 g F, 50 g CH

1 Separate the eggs. Beat the egg yolks in a bowl until very frothy. Gradually add the sugar, vanilla sugar, almonds, lemon zest, lemon juice, orange zest and stir until creamy. Add the flour and salt to the mixture and stir thoroughly. Beat the egg whites until stiff and fold into the cake mixture with a fork until it forms a smooth batter.

2 Pour the batter into a greased loaf pan (25 cm) and bake for an hour in the oven at 170 °C (Gas Mark 3, fan oven 150 °C). Turn the cake out onto a wire rack and sprinkle with icing sugar.

Ricotta ice cream
with espresso

Serves 4

125 ml espresso coffee

500 g ricotta

100 g sugar

4 egg yolks

3 tbsp cream

1 tsp vanilla sugar

4 tbsp Marsala

2 tbsp cocoa powder

Preparation time: 15 minutes
(plus freezing time)
Per serving approx. 428 kcal/
1792 kJ
20 g P, 28 g F, 33 g CH

1 Leave the espresso to cool. Strain the ricotta through a sieve and mix with the espresso. Stir the sugar and egg yolks together until frothy. Beat the cream until stiff, then stir in the vanilla sugar and Marsala. Mix the espresso and ricotta mixture and the egg froth together, then fold in the cream. Pour the mixture into a bowl or rectangular dish and cover with cling film. Freeze for approx. 3 hours until set.

2 You can put the ricotta ice cream into small bowls using an ice cream scoop, cut into slices or spoon onto waffles. Serve sprinkled with cocoa powder.

Cannoli
with ricotta filling

Serves 4

25 g butter
125 g sugar
2 eggs
2 ½ tbsp milk
3 tbsp vanilla sugar
pinch of salt
150 g wheat flour
oil for deep frying
500 g Ricotta
2 tbsp orange liqueur
100 g mixed chopped
    candied orange and
    lemon peel
50 g candied cherries
90 g chopped dark chocolate
icing sugar

Preparation time: 30 minutes
(plus cooling time)
Per serving approx. 863 kcal/
3613 kJ
25 g P, 39 g F, 101 g CH

1 Mix the butter with 25 g sugar, 1 egg, 2 ½ tablespoons of milk, 2 tablespoons of vanilla sugar, salt and flour until it forms a smooth dough. Cover and stand in a cool place for 2 hours.

2 Roll the dough out until it is 2 mm thick, then cut into 16 squares (12 x 12 cm). Place bamboo or metal rods (15 cm long, 2 cm diameter) diagonally across the pieces of dough, wrap the opposite corners around the rods and brush with the whisked egg. Deep fry the cannoli in the hot oil until golden brown, then remove the rods and leave the rolls of pastry to dry and cool.

3 Mix the ricotta with the orange liqueur, candied fruits, the rest of the sugar, the vanilla sugar and the chocolate. Fill the cannoli with the mixture and sprinkle with icing sugar.

Crespelle
with strawberries

Serves 4

3 eggs

250 ml milk

5 tbsp mineral water

100 g flour

80 g sugar

1 pinch of salt

5 tbsp clarified butter

2 tbsp butter

120 ml white wine

120 ml orange liqueur

300 g strawberries

zest of ½ untreated lemon

Preparation time: 20 minutes
Per serving approx.
1147 kcal/4802 kJ
11 g P, 91 g F, 55 g CH

1 Mix the eggs with the milk and 5 tablespoons of mineral water in a bowl. Stir in the flour, gradually add 30 g sugar and then the pinch of salt. Mix everything until it forms a smooth batter and leave to rest for 10 minutes. Heat the clarified butter in a pan and fry the batter in batches to make thin pancakes. Keep warm.

2 Heat the butter in a pan and caramelise the rest of the sugar.

3 Gradually add the white wine and orange liqueur and bring to a boil, stirring, until it forms a syrup. Cut the strawberries into small pieces. Add to the pan and heat through. Spoon onto the pancakes while still warm, scatter over the zest and fold the pancakes.

Lemon semifreddo
with rum

Serves 4

250 ml mandarin juice
250 ml orange juice
250 ml grapefruit juice
125 ml lime juice
200 g sugar
100 ml rum
orange zest

Preparation time: 20 minutes
(plus freezing time)
Per serving approx. 377 kcal/
1578 kJ
1 g P, 1 g F, 72 g CH

1 Pour the freshly pressed juices through a strainer and mix with 250 ml water. Add the sugar and rum and mix everything together well. Pour into a metal bowl and leave to set for several hours in the freezer.

2 Stir with a fork or whisk several times while freezing. Serve garnished with orange zest.

Panna cotta
Italian cream pudding

Serves 4

1 vanilla pod
400 ml cream
40 g sugar
3 gelatine leaves

Preparation time: 20 minutes
(plus cooling time)
Per serving approx. 330 kcal/
1380 kJ
4 g P, 30 g F, 13 g CH

1 Slice the vanilla pod lengthways and scrape out the seeds with a sharp knife. Heat the cream with the vanilla seeds, vanilla pod and sugar in a bowl inside a bain-marie and simmer for at least 10 minutes. Soak the gelatine in cold water.

2 Remove the pot from the heat and take out the vanilla pod. Squeeze out the gelatine leaves and stir them into the cream. Return the pot to the heat and dissolve the gelatine while stirring the mixture over a low heat.

3 Rinse out 4 dessert bowls with cold water, fill with the cooked cream and leave to set in the fridge for 4–5 hours. Turn onto dessert plates before serving and garnish to taste.

216   *Desserts and sweet dishes*

Tiramisu
the classic Italian dessert

Serves 4

2 egg yolks

2 tbsp sugar

350 g Mascarpone

2 tbsp Amaretto

100 g sponge fingers

50 ml cold espresso coffee

2-3 tbsp unsweetened cocoa

Preparation time: 20 minutes
(plus cooling time)
Per serving approx. 520 kcal/
2170 kJ
7 g P, 42 g F, 28 g CH

1 Put the egg yolks and sugar in a bowl and use an electric whisk to beat the mixture until it is frothy. Add the Mascarpone spoonful by spoonful and add Amaretto to taste, stirring constantly.

2 Cover the bottom of a flat baking dish or serving bowl with half of the sponge fingers. Drizzle some espresso over the top, followed by a layer of half of the mascarpone cream. Follow this with another layer of sponge fingers, more espresso and the other half of the mascarpone cream.

3 Cover the tiramisu and leave in the fridge for at least 4 hours so that the flavours can develop well. Sprinkle cocoa powder over the dessert before serving.

Baklava
a Middle Eastern speciality

Makes 10 pieces

200 g pistachio nuts
100 g peeled almonds
450 g sugar
1 tsp cardamom seeds
1 tsp cinnamon
125 g butter
750 g yufka dough
1 tsp lemon juice
½ tsp ground cardamom
1 tbsp rose water

Preparation time: 1 hour
(plus baking time)
Per piece approx. 1413 kcal/
5933 kJ
30 g P, 90 g F, 123 g CH

1 Grind the pistachio nuts, almonds, 150 g sugar and the cardamom seeds in a food processor and mix in the cinnamon. Melt the butter.

2 Grease a rectangular baking dish with a little butter, cut out three layers of yufka dough and brush with butter. Place the dough in the dish and spread with the nut mixture. Place two more layers of dough on top, then add another layer of nuts. Repeat this process, finishing off with three layers of buttered yufka dough.

3 Cut the dough into diamond shapes, brush with the rest of the butter and bake at 180 °C (Gas Mark 4, fan oven 160 °C) on the middle tray of the oven for 35–40 minutes.

4 While the pastries are baking, put the rest of the sugar in a pot with 500 ml water and bring to a boil. Stir in the lemon juice and ground cardamom and pour in the rose water while the mixture is still boiling. Take the baklava out of the oven, pour over the syrup and cut up the diamond-shaped pastries.

Apple rolls
with almond caramel

Serves 4

750 g sharp apples
2 tbsp butter
125 g sugar
125 g flaked almonds
10–12 sheets filo or yufka
  pastry
2 egg yolks
oil for deep frying
icing sugar
baking parchment

Preparation time: 20 minutes
(plus cooking and baking time)
Per serving approx. 635 kcal/
2667 kJ
10 g P, 45 g F, 49 g CH

1 Peel and core the apples and cut into small dice. Heat the butter and sauté the apples with 3 tablespoons of sugar for approx. 8 minutes, until the pieces are tender and any liquid has completely boiled off.

2 Toast the almond flakes in a dry pan until golden brown, then sprinkle over the rest of the sugar and caramelise, stirring constantly, until light brown. Spoon the mixture onto baking parchment and leave to cool, then chop into small pieces.

3 Cut the sheets of pastry in half diagonally. Stir the almond caramel into the apple sauce. Spoon the apple and caramel filling onto the long side of the halved sheets of dough, leaving one edge free. Brush the edges of the pastry with whisked egg yolk.

4 Fold both of the outer corners inwards over the filling. Roll up the pastry sheets towards the top and deep fry in the hot oil for about a minute, until golden brown.

5 Remove the rolls from the pan and leave to dry on kitchen paper. Dredge with icing sugar before serving.

Apricot and nut skewers
with chocolate

Serves 4

12 ripe yet firm apricots

125 g butter

4 tbsp sugar

pinch of vanilla sugar

50 g grated dark chocolate

12 halved almonds, walnuts
or cashew nuts

4 grilling skewers

a little icing sugar

Preparation time: 25 minutes
(plus baking time)
Per serving approx. 520 kcal/
2184 kJ
7 g P, 41 g F, 31 g CH

1 Pre-heat the grill to 200 °C (Gas Mark 6, fan oven 180 °C). Wash the apricots, rub dry and remove the stones from the fruit, cutting a small notch at the base of the leaves and carefully pulling out the stone, making sure that the fruit remains intact.

2 Mix the soft butter with the sugar and vanilla sugar in a bowl, and fold in the grated chocolate. Stuff each apricot with an almond, walnut or cashew nut. Add a little of the butter mixture to close the opening.

3 Toss the apricots in the rest of the butter mixture. Thread 2–3 apricots onto each skewer, depending on their size, and place on a grill tray. Grill in the oven for approx. 10 minutes.

4 Remove from the oven, sprinkle with icing sugar and serve hot. These apricot and nut skewers also go well with vanilla ice cream.

 Honey and almond biscuits

Makes 20 biscuits

½ tsp bicarbonate of soda

juice and zest of 1 untreated orange

150 ml olive oil

325 g honey

60 ml Greek brandy

1 ½ tsp cinnamon

400 g flour

3 tsp baking powder

pinch of salt

120 g sugar

100 g chopped almonds

Preparation time: 1 hour
Per biscuit approx. 217 kcal/ 911 kJ
3 g P, 8 g F, 32 g CH

1 Stir the bicarbonate of soda into the orange juice. Mix the olive oil with 75 g honey until smooth, then pour in the Greek brandy, 1/2 teaspoon of cinnamon and the orange juice.

2 Mix the flour with the baking powder and sieve into the olive oil and honey mixture, stirring. Add salt and knead the dough well using a mixer. Add the orange zest and knead the dough until smooth.

3 Pre-heat the oven to 180 °C (Gas Mark 4, fan oven 160 °C). Pull little bits off the dough and make oval or round biscuit shapes. Place these on a greased baking tray.

4 Press every biscuit flat with a fork. Bake for approx. 20–25 minutes in the oven. Turn onto a wire rack and leave to cool.

5 Mix the rest of the honey with the sugar and 150 ml water and bring to a boil in a pot, then simmer for approx. 5 minutes. Lower the biscuits into the syrup in batches and leave to soak for approx. 2 minutes, then remove and scatter with almonds and the rest of the cinnamon.

Date cake
with orange liqueur

**For 1 springform baking tin
(diameter 26 cm)**

400 g fresh dates

150 g almonds

150 g sugar

3 tbsp butter

4 eggs

1 sachet bourbon vanilla
   sugar or the seeds from
   1 vanilla pod

3 tbsp cornflour

20 ml orange liqueur

butter for greasing

icing sugar for sprinkling

Preparation time: 20 minutes
(plus baking time)
Per cake approx. 299 kcal/1256 kJ
6 g P, 12 g F, 42 g CH

1 Pre-heat the oven to 225 °C (Gas Mark 7, fan oven 200 °C). Wash the dates, remove the seeds and finely chop the flesh. Plunge the almonds into boiling water and leave to stand for 1 minute. Drain away the water and remove the skins from the almonds.

2 Place the almonds on a baking tray and leave to dry for approx. 3 minutes in the oven at 200 °C (Gas Mark 6, fan oven 180 °C). Leave to cool slightly, then crush with ⅔ of the sugar in a mortar or blend to a fine purée.

3 Melt the butter. Separate the eggs. Mix the egg yolks with the rest of the sugar and the vanilla sugar or the vanilla seeds, and stir until frothy. Stir in the cornflour.

4 Add the finely chopped dates, the almond mixture, melted butter and the orange liqueur to the egg and sugar mixture, and carefully mix together. Beat the egg whites until they form stiff peaks and gradually fold into the date mixture.

5 Grease a springform baking tin (diameter 26 cm) with butter and pour in the date mixture. Bake the cake for approx. 20 minutes. After the baking time is up, reduce the temperature to 180 °C (Gas Mark 4, fan oven 160 °C) and bake the cake for another 20–25 minutes. Take out of the oven, leave to cool and serve sprinkled with icing sugar.

Crêpes Suzette
French orange pancakes

Serves 4

2 eggs
200 ml milk
salt
80 g wheat flour
220 g sugar
100 g butter
6 untreated oranges
4 tbsp orange liqueur
(e.g. Cointreau)

Preparation time: 40 minutes
(plus cooking time)
Per serving approx. 660 kcal/
2760 kJ
9 g P, 26 g F, 90 g CH

1 Whisk the eggs with the milk. Add the salt, flour and 2 tablespoons of sugar, and mix everything to a smooth batter. Froth up half of the butter in a pan, and when it is golden brown, stir into the batter.

2 To make the sauce, wash 3 oranges in hot water and remove the peel in fine strips. Squeeze these 3 oranges and mix the juice with the orange peel and the rest of the sugar in a pot. Bring to a boil and reduce down to a runny syrup over a high heat.

3 Peel the remaining oranges, completely removing the white skin. Cut the segments from their membranes. Collect any juice and add to the syrup.

4 Froth up some butter in 2 coated pans. Pour a ladleful of batter into each, cook the crêpes on both sides until golden brown and then place on a wire rack. Cover with a tea towel and keep warm. Make 12 golden brown crêpes in this way.

5 When all of the crêpes are done divide the orange segments between them. Fold the crêpes up and place next to each other in 1 or 2 pans. Spoon the sugar syrup and orange liqueur over the top. Warm everything through once again and flambé by setting fire to the liqueur with a long match. Serve immediately.

Mousse au chocolat
French chocolate cream

Serves 4

100 g dark chocolate

2 eggs

1 tbsp sugar

250 ml cream

4 decorative chocolate
  hearts

Preparation time: 20 minutes
(plus cooking and cooling time)
Per serving approx. 390 kcal/
1630 kJ
7 g P, 33 g F, 17 g CH

1 Chop the chocolate finely with a large kitchen knife. Melt the chocolate pieces in a bowl in a bain-marie, stirring often. As soon as the chocolate has melted, take the pot off the heat and leave to cool a little.

2 Beat and separate the eggs. Pour the egg whites into a bowl and use an electric whisk to beat them until they form stiff peaks.

3 Mix the egg yolks with the sugar in another bowl until frothy, then carefully stir in the warm, melted chocolate.

4 Beat the cream with an electric whisk until stiff. When the chocolate has cooled a little, fold in 1 tablespoon of the egg whites. Continue to fold in the egg whites and cream in spoonfuls. Do not stir too vigorously, as otherwise the egg whites and cream will collapse.

5 Pour the mousse into cold, rinsed dessert bowls and leave to cool in the fridge for 3–4 hours until they are firm. Place the decorative chocolate hearts and fresh fruit on top before serving, and dust with icing sugar.

Crème brûlée
with fruit

Serves 4

125 ml milk

125 ml cream

2 eggs

2 egg yolks

65 g icing sugar

seeds from ½ vanilla pod

6 tbsp sugar for baking

fresh seasonal fruit

Preparation time: 15 minutes
(plus baking and cooling time)
Per serving approx. 292 kcal/
1226 kJ
7 g P, 17 g F, 26 g CH

1 Pre-heat the oven to 150 °C (Gas Mark 2, fan oven 125 °C). Mix the milk with the cream, eggs, egg yolks, icing sugar and vanilla seeds.

2 Pour the egg mixture into four small, flat, oven-proof dishes and place in a large baking tin filled with water. Bake in the oven for 35 minutes, until the mixture has set.

3 Take the dishes out of the oven, leave to cool and leave in the fridge overnight. Sprinkle the *crème* with sugar shortly before serving and place under a hot grill until the sugar begins to brown. Fresh fruit makes a good accompaniment.

Ice cream soufflé
with orange liqueur

Serves 4–6

150 ml cream

250 g sugar

6 eggs

50 g ground almonds

100 ml orange liqueur

greaseproof paper

4 tsp chopped almonds

Preparation time: 30 minutes
(plus cooking and freezing time)
Per serving approx. 433 kcal/
1818 kJ
9 g P, 18 g F, 47 g CH

1 Beat the cream until stiff. Place the sugar in a pot with 250 ml water and boil down, stirring, until it forms a syrup.

2 Separate the eggs. Beat the egg whites until they form stiff peaks and slowly stir in the sugar syrup.

3 Beat the egg yolks in a pot with a little water until they are frothy – they should not clot. Fold the sugar and egg whites into the egg yolk mixture.

4 Toast the ground almonds in a dry pan. Stir the almonds and orange liqueur into the egg mixture. Leave to cool and mix with the cream.

5 Line a soufflé dish with greaseproof paper, allowing more room towards the top. Pour the mixture over the edge and leave to freeze for at least 6 hours. Remove the paper before serving and garnish with chopped almonds.

Index